Yesterday's Boys

ROBERT TAYLOR

Order this book online at www.trafford.com
or email orders@trafford.com

Most Trafford titles are also available at major online book retailers.

Print information available on the last page.

ISBN: 978-1-4907-5813-8 (sc)
ISBN: 978-1-4907-5812-1 (hc)
ISBN: 978-1-4907-5811-4 (e)

Library of Congress Control Number: 2015905434

Trafford rev. 04/24/2015

 www.trafford.com
North America & international
toll-free: 1 888 232 4444 (USA & Canada)
fax: 812 355 4082

Contents

Introduction

I have always found humor in the simple things in life. That is one of the reasons I decided to write this book. I also wanted to tell a few stories about my family, relatives, and friends. I wanted my children and grandchildren to read my version of life in the country and the years to follow.

There were many sad times, but there were many more fun times. Times free of guns, knives, and drugs. You will find this book an easy read and straight from the heart. It is a compilation of true stories. I do not know any other way. The most heartwarming comment I received after my first book was "When I read your book, it was just like you were talking to me." I was overjoyed by this comment as that is exactly what I wanted to portray.

As you go from cover to cover, you will surely be reminded of the fun you had as a child and as you grew older. It will give you an opportunity to relive part of your past. Remembering the good times is so much fun.

When I grow up I want to be a little boy. (Joseph Heller)

Days with My Mother

Jean MacLean Stewart Taylor.
Our beautiful Mother.

I did not get to share much time with my mother. She passed away when I was only six years old, but it is amazing how much I do remember. My mother was a Stewart and was born on Stewart hill, near Upper Musquodoboit. I was also born there in a house very near to my grandparents. Members of our family were certainly country folks as we could see very few homes from where we lived, and each house was quite a distance away. Even when my mother was quite ill, I was too young to realize just what was going on around me. My brothers and sisters were older, and I suppose they realized she was not going to be with us for very long. When my siblings were at school, I had my mom all to myself. She would tell me stories and would give me little chores to do to help out.

One of the chores I had was to take the potato peelings out to the yard for the cow that was always close by. My first trip was a real thriller. She told me to take the peelings out in the plum basket, which was used for that purpose, and just dump them on the ground in front of the cow (the cow's name was Aggie). Things would have been fine, but Aggie saw me coming and started to move my way in a hurried fashion. I was scared out of my wits and started to run toward the old woodhouse as fast as I could with Aggie right at my heels. When I reached the woodhouse door, I saw a pile of wood in the back corner. I ran inside and climbed up as high as I could get on the wood. Old Aggie followed me right into the shed, and I am sure the screams were heard for miles around. My mother came out and very calmly told me to dump the basket and Aggie would leave me alone. What a relief to see that old cow move her attention away from me and start eating the peelings. I remember mother holding me until I started to breathe like a normal child again.

One warm summer day, it had started to rain quite hard and I was upset as I wanted to play outside. Mother suggested I go out anyway as it was warm and the rain would feel nice. I could not believe what she was saying until she convinced me to try it. She found an old pair of short pants and dressed me in them for my day in the rain. I went to the door rather reluctantly and stepped out. Much to my surprise, it was warm and the drops of rain felt very nice. As it started to rain even harder, I began to run around the house and found myself laughing and really enjoying my new experience. Later in life, I had an opportunity to convince my own children to do the same thing. It was an exhilarating event for them as well.

My mother was a schoolteacher in her early years, but raising children became her full-time job. What a job it must have been. To say she had the bare essentials would be a real stretch. I remember during the winter months and the others were off to school, she would spend her spare time keeping me company. On one occasion, she agreed to let me go to school with the others. It was to be a special day, as there would be a basket social. My mother prepared a lunch for me to take, and she put it in a chocolate box. I was really excited and could not wait for morning to come. When I looked out the next day, it was snowing very hard and my mother decided I was too young to brave the storm. She finally got me calmed down by promising me she would help me eat my lunch in front of the old kitchen stove where it was nice and warm. We did have lunch together that day, as we did most days, but this day was very special because it was our own social event. I did not get to school that day, but I had a great time. I still have a vivid picture of that old chocolate box in my mind.

On another occasion, I was to accompany her to the village so she could attend a funeral for a Mr. Henry. I was to go and stay at another house where there would be others to play with. The day of the funeral, my mother was too sick to attend, so I stayed home with her. I was quite upset because of the change in our plans and told my mother, "The next time Mr. Henry dies, I am going!" I later learned about this story from an older lady who thought it was very funny.

I mentioned that my mother was a teacher, but I did not mention that out of a family of nine, there were six of them who taught school. Their mother was also a teacher. Not bad for a farming family.

There were a lot of stories my mother told us, but most of them have been lost or hidden deep in my mind. I do remember her telling us about one of their long walks home from school on a very snowy day. She was walking with her oldest sister Elsie. They started up the long hill toward their parents' house. It started to snow very hard, and there was already snow on the ground. To make matters much worse, the wind started to blow. They still had about a quarter of a mile to go, and visibility was almost nil. They continued on until they ran into the old pasture fence. They knew that if they followed it uphill, they would come to the house. They still could not see very well but held on to each other with one hand and held the fence with the other. After what must have been a long struggle, they arrived home to a warm house and probably nervous parents. In those days, snow days had a much different meaning.

I remember the day our mother went to the hospital. It was a sad day for all of us. That day would be the last time I saw her alive. She hugged me and told me she was going to Truro to the hospital. My grandmother was there that day and corrected her by saying, "You are going to Halifax." Mother was very ill, and I could not understand why they would not just let her think she was going to Truro. She passed away a short time after that, and our family had to face the world without her. These were sad times, I tell you, but we did our best to keep going. Over the years, we did quite well and still think of her often.

I have many fond memories of my mother, but there are many things I wish I could have told her. To those of you who still have an opportunity to speak with your parents, please do so as often as you can. Don't wait too long as time goes by all too quickly.

My Sisters Mildred Frances and Thelma.

Rob on Mower.

The Days on Stewart Hill

Stewart hill is situated in Halifax County, Nova Scotia. It is part of the Village of Upper Musquodoboit. As you can imagine, it is on a hill overlooking the village below. In years gone by, it was mostly farmland, and many families made their home there. When settlers first came to the Musquodoboit Valley, they must have been afraid of flooding conditions, as several of them carved out their farms on the hills. In later years, the lower land was tilled and no doubt the farmers found the soil much more fertile.

By the time I was born in 1938, many of the farms had been sold or abandoned, and families living there were few and far between. My grandfather Stewart farmed there until his death in 1939. The farmhouse where I was born was owned by Jeff Stewart, who moved down farther in the valley and rented the house to my mother and father. My father was not a farmer, but he had a cow, a few hens, and on one occasion, a pig. We got by as well as a family of seven could in those days. I can't remember not having enough to eat or being so cold I suffered from it. I think that overall, I was very fortunate to have loving parents and great siblings.

There were many happy days for us on that old farm in spite of the hardships my parents must have endured. I was too young to feel the pain of the hard times, and I am thankful I enjoyed the good times. I do remember when my mother passed away, and this was a very sad time in the lives of all of us. Due to the difference in our ages, I am sure we all felt a unique loss. Our mother had been ill for quite some time, but she always had a sweet smile for all of us. Being the youngest, I suppose I drew a lot of attention and caused her more pain than I would like to admit. I have very fond memories of our short time together. There are several stories I will relate later on about our time together and how she watched over me.

The Warplanes

was too young to fully understand the war years, but I did live through part of it and come to develop a fear of the unknown. I remember the blackouts we had at night, and even at a young age, I could not see the need for them on our old farm. Shades would be drawn in every window, and the old oil lamp would be turned down low. We lived in a rural farm area, and the nearest house was a quarter of a mile away.

I guess it was part of the times, and everyone had at least a small part to play in securing our safety. We had a radio that we could listen to when absolutely necessary, and that was not very often. It was mostly for the war news (not too good for a five-year-old boy). I remember the coupons my parents received in order to buy certain items. I don't know what actual products were rationed for sure, but I think sugar and gasoline were two. It was a life I was born into, and I did not realize how bad it was until the later years.

It was slightly before this time that two of my brothers, Stewart and Keith, joined the Boy Scouts of Canada. They would walk down to the village on a regular basis and take part in the scouting activities. One of the things they learned was the Morse code. This was a signaling practice that was very important in those times. They became very proficient at this, and Stewart started to send messages to a friend of his down in the village. They both had flashlights, and they used them to communicate in code with one another.

My brother had an old tree he could climb, giving him a straight line of sight to his friend down in the village. As the crow flies, I suppose, they were a mile and one half apart. I am not sure how long this continued each night or how many nights they flashed their lights.

It was not too long, however, until some of the local people saw the lights, and the stories spread through the village. I am sure none of them understood the code, but at least one person was sure there were spies in the area. They even threatened to summon the police to come and check it out. My father heard about the threat and contacted the proper authorities right away. That ended the worries, and I suppose by this time the boys had tired of their little exercise and went on to something else. Stewart joined the navy later on, and his friend Keith studied to become a minister. Stewart left the navy after a few years and went to work for the Canadian National Railways. He would later transfer to Yarmouth with the *Bluenose* ferry. Keith left the ministry and started teaching. He would end up in Australia (too far away to send messages by flashlight).

It was when they were both in their eighty-fifth year that they would meet via the telephone and talk for almost an hour, one in Yarmouth, Nova Scotia, and the other in Australia. This time, I doubt if there were any complaints from the local people. How times have changed.

One of my wartime memories was about the warplanes that flew over the farmland where we lived. I am not sure how many times they flew over, but I do remember the first time I saw them. I was outside messing around one warm sunny day and decided I would go check out an old horse-drawn mower. It was in the field about a hundred yards from the house. I was sure my mother was watching, as she never let me out of her sight if she could help it. She never mentioned it to me, but I know she had her way of protecting her little boy.

I crawled up in the iron seat and was pretending I was driving a horse and mowing hay. I heard a strange roaring noise behind me, but nothing was in sight. I looked all around and nothing. The sound got louder and louder, but I still had no idea where the noise was coming from. Then in a flash, I saw them just at the top of the long hill that reached from our house up a gradual incline for a long distance and then drop off out of sight. There were three airplanes flying my way. They were so close to the ground that the grass was waving under their wings. I was so frightened that I jumped off the mower and crawled under the seat and lay on the grass. They flew down toward the house and then off into the air again. They seemed to go up so far I could hardly see them. In a few minutes, they would do the same maneuver over again. I was still scared, but I was very excited as well. I think it was during that short period of time that I became very interested in airplanes. They would come on several occasions after that, and I would marvel at those planes and their occupants. I would later wonder how many of those young pilots would go off to war and never return.

There is a very interesting sequel to this story. I was later to find out the names of the planes, where they were made, and where they flew from and talked to one of the pilots—a rare opportunity.

A very good friend of mine, Mr. Edgil Dauphinee, was an instructor during the first part of the war. I have known him for several years and have often played the fiddle with

him. I did not know until very recently that the planes I was so afraid of came from the Stanley airport in Nova Scotia. They were there at Stewart hill to practice emergency landing. That explains the grass waving under their wings. Edgil also told me he had flown in that area and could have been one of the pilots on that very hill, and if he was there the first day I saw them, he was one of the pilots who scared me so bad.

The planes I refer to were Tiger Moths. They were built for wartime and had two open cockpits. They were single-engine planes with double wings.

It Started with the Small Potatoes

The days on Stewart hill were special. There are many stories and not enough time to do them justice, but another comes to mind about my brother Keith. He had been given a chore to do for our mother. He was splitting wood for the stove. Another brother, Malcolm, decided he would create a little havoc and started throwing small potatoes at Keith. These potatoes were the ones that were so small they were left on the ground after the others were picked. Malcolm (we called him Mac and a few other names as well) was a pest at times, and this was one of those times. Keith took it for a while and then started to reciprocate by giving Mac a cuff on the ear. Mother came out of the house and caught Keith in the act.

Mother was not pleased with his actions and told him so. He told her he had his fill with Mac throwing potatoes at him and if that was the way it was going to be, he would just simply leave home. We were not quite sure what else may have been said, but Keith did leave and go down to the village. He went to see a friend of his and asked to stay all night (in modern times, that would be called a sleepover). No one else knew where he was or what had happened. Can you imagine how my mother must have felt that night not knowing where he was? Phones were few and far between, and communication was impossible unless you were face-to-face.

He stayed all night with his friend and went to school from there the next day. My sisters and brothers told him he better get home as our mother was very worried. At this point, I am sure he wished he was home, but his pride made him finish out the school day and then go home.

When Keith told me this story many years later, he was telling me with a tear in his eye. He knew he had hurt our mother very much and probably never got to tell her how sorry he was. Sometimes we get provoked by one person and we end up hurting another.

Keith has always been a real gentleman and worshipped his parents. He left school when he was fifteen years old to drive a truck so he could help support our family in tough times. He worked in the limestone pits and did not have to drive on the main roads, thus no license was required. He has certainly paid his dues over the years.

Riding a Horse

It was on my grandfather's farm that I would get my first horseback ride. My cousin Evans Stewart put me on the old horse they had and made me feel like a king. He led the horse to the pasture up over the hill for a few sticks of wood and let me ride on the horse all the way. I don't think anyone else knew about this ride except Evans and me. Evans was like a friendly giant to me. He was well over six feet tall and was as gentle as a lamb. He is gone now, but I will always remember him and the great ride I had.

It was at this farm as well that I had my first experience with a serious accident. I was not involved, but I did get to see the whole messy scene. Fred Stewart, who was a brother of Evans, was playing with the milk separator. For those of you who are not familiar with this machine, it was quite simply used to separate the cream from milk. It was a hand-operated machine that was quite easily used by one person. On this occasion, my cousin Fred was playing with it and not doing anything constructive. There was a small shaft that protruded from the base of the machine. When the crank was turned to full speed, the shaft reached very high rpms. This shaft had a slot in it that normally turned the main part of the separator. Fred found a tin can cover and folded it in the middle to resemble a half moon. He placed the cover in the slot on top of the shaft and proceeded to turn the crank as fast as he could. This caused the can cover to spin around at very high rpms as well. In just a few seconds, Fred had it turning at full speed and then the can cover flew off and hit Fred in the forearm. The blood flow appeared almost instantly. I was scared he would die in front of me.

My aunt Bessy and my grandmother came to his rescue and took him into the kitchen and put him on the old couch. I understand my brother Keith was there as well and, because of his Boy Scouts training, helped stop the flow of blood. He then ran down the hill to the nearest house with a phone and called the local doctor. He was soon fixed up to work again, but I doubt if he ever touched the separator unless it was to actually separate the cream.

That group of cousins was always close to me, and I developed a strong bond that still holds true to this day. Part of that family has gone now, but I have vivid memories. One of the younger children in the family, who was near my age, Avis Stewart, passed away when she was about six or seven. We played together on Stewart hill on many occasions. My fondest memory of her was making snow angels in the winter. When she died, I could not understand why she had to leave. That is a part of life that reveals few answers.

Enjoy the little things in life, for one day they will be big things.

Mildred and Malcolm (The Twins).

My Mother's Family. Jean, Brydon, Grandfather, Grandmother, Verna, Elsie. Front Row, Ola, Byron, Owen, Elmer and Bobby. About 1924, this is my best guest.

The Wagon Ride

I was not involved in this adventure, but I understand it was quite a ride. My oldest brother Stewart had somehow come across an old buggy that had seen better days. I will explain the circumstances as best as I can, but I was too young at the time to pay close attention. I should explain first that Stewart was one of the best people I ever knew to build something out of a pile of rubble. We had all learned this from our father, as he was very capable of doing this, and quite often it was out of necessity. Stewart, however, must have learned well as he was the best and is still that way at eighty-seven years of age.

Our father had bought an old barn that was just up the hill from the farm we lived on. He tore the old barn down and brought the boards back to our house to rebuild. In the barn, there was an old horse-drawn buggy that Stewart took a keen liking to. I am sure he had visions of creating a beautiful carriage. Father gave him permission to bring it home. I guess it was payment for all the hard work of tearing the old barn apart.

I am not sure of the events that followed, but I will try to explain them as I remember. I mentioned that the wagon had been horse drawn, but Stewart had other ideas. He decided to rebuild it so it would in some way resemble a car. He geared up makeshift brakes on the back wheels and ropes tied to front axles to steer with. I am not sure how long it took to do all this, but I rather doubt it would pass today's safety Inspection. Then came the first test run. For this big adventure, he brought together three more of the best boys on Stewart hill to do the first run (there were only six boys on the whole hill at that time). Stewart was certainly the man in charge. He had brother Keith and two cousins, Fred and Evans Stewart. The plan was quite simple. Stewart and Fred, the two oldest, would man the steering. Keith and Evans who were in the rear would control the brakes. They were off to roll down Stewart hill. Most of you will not realize the magnitude of this journey until you understand the hill I'm referring to. The Stewart hill road began at the main highway that ran through the village. It went up a steep hill that was quite crooked, continued on in a big loop and back down to the main road, joining it about a mile and one half from the starting point. I estimate a total of two and a half miles.

The boys decided to test their contraption on the steepest end. They would push it quite a long distance to reach their intended launch site. They reached the hill, and all hands jumped on board. The horseless carriage started to roll down the hill. In a very short time, they were speeding down the hill. A cry for brakes was soon given. When the boys at the back tried to do this, a part of the braking system had fallen out of place. Stewart, the captain, turned quickly to look; and in doing so, he must have pulled on the rope he was steering with. This sent the craft racing into the ditch. The force of the impact caused the boys in the rear to fly right over the front seat and into the woods. I don't believe any of the boys were hurt. It was a miracle that they went off the road where they did. For those of you who know the hill well, try to imagine rolling down that hill all the way in a worn-out buggy. A video of this event would be priceless.

I mentioned that I was too young to understand much about this buggy ride, but I did get a chance later to learn firsthand just how much

Stewart wanted to improve his pride and joy. The ride down the hill did not deter his desire to make things work. I am not sure how long he worked on the buggy, but he did put a makeshift steering wheel on it. And I understand he intended to put a gas engine in it for power.

On one of his test runs (it may have been his last), he gave me a chance to help him test it. I am guessing I would have been four or five at the time. He gave me very explicit instructions on how to steer the vehicle. He told me that all I had to do was steer. Somehow we got the wagon up on the hill facing the house. This hill was not very steep, so I was not in any real danger. (That is what he told me at the time.) This was the same hill I got my thrill and scare from the Tiger Moth planes. There was a bit of a lane that went from the house up the hill. There was another lane that went in a right angle from the house out to the old main road. We were at the top of the hill when he gave me the final instructions. "All you have to do is steer, I will do the rest." He gave the wagon a little push to get it rolling, and he followed along behind. It was fun. I was very young, but I was steering. I think he had geared up an old wheel off a wheelbarrow, or perhaps it was from some other farm implement. It did not matter to me at the time; I was in heaven. I was to let it go straight until I got to the lane from the house to the road. At this point, I was to turn sharp left and continue out the lane.

As I made the turn, I looked out the lane and saw there was a car coming in the lane. All of a sudden I could hear shoes dragging in the gravel. It was a noise I will never forget. Stewart had a hold on the back of the wagon and was dragging both feet. The brakes worked that time. He got the wagon slowed down and told me to steer it into the grass on the side of the lane. The car that was coming in was that of our local minister. I am sure they had a laugh when everything came to a stop. I don't remember the wagon after that day. Perhaps he was encouraged to get rid of it. I think he left to join the navy shortly after that. Stewart is my oldest brother and has always been someone I looked up to.

He had been working for a few weeks in the summer in Upper Stewiacke. When he came home from there, he brought ice cream for the family. It was a hot day, and he had between five and six miles to walk. When he got home, the ice cream was mostly melted. I loved it. I had never had any before, and to me, it was just fine. From that day on, I liked my ice cream soft. When I was a few years older, I had my first ice cream cone. We had gone down to visit my grandparents in Wittenburg. On the way home, Father stopped at a little canteen and got us all an Ice-cream. After I had been eating for a short time, I noticed that my brothers and sisters were all watching me and laughing. I did not know that the cone itself was edible. I must have been a sight trying to get the ice cream out and not eat the cone.

In later years, I would learn that I caused a good deal of concern when it was time for me to be born. Frances had made plans to go down to the village after school on Friday to visit a good friend of hers. She was excited as these people had a boardinghouse and a restaurant. She even made plans to stay all night. Today, that would be a sleepover. My father came that day to pick her up to take her home to see her new brother. I don't think she was overly pleased.

My sister Mildred went to visit my aunt Elsie that weekend and missed the whole show. She did tell me many years later that it was a beautiful time of year and she enjoyed the pretty flowers.

When Frances was about four years old, she went to our dad just after supper one evening and said, "Come on, Cliff, it is time to go milk the cow." In those days, it was forbidden to talk to your father like that, but I am sure her father had a chuckle. In those days, we learned very quickly to respect our parents and be very careful how we talked to them. Once we were out of their hearing range, it was sometimes a little different.

Brother Stewart years later on his way to town.

17

Aggie's Calves

It was a warm summer evening, and our precious Aggie had not come home from the pasture. Aggie was our cow. We named her after the lady my dad bought her from. I was old enough by this time that I had grown quite fond of her. I was also concerned that she had not come home. My dad decided to go look for her and take me along with him. I think that more of the family went along with us, but I am not sure which ones tagged along. The pasture was on our grandfather's property and was a long walk for a young boy.

It seemed to take a long time to walk across the fields and up into the pasture. After a farther walk, we came to a few trees and found her there. She had two beautiful calves with her. I was totally surprised at this discovery because I was not aware of her condition. I am sure everyone else knew the reason for her delay, but no one expected two calves. I will never forget the evening coming home from the pasture, which seemed like such a short distance. As soon as Dad got one of the calves on its feet and walking, the other calf and Aggie joined us. I was so proud of our family. Needless to say, I was very upset when Dad told us he was going to sell the new calves.

I am not sure how long it was before they went to the new owners, but we all realized we could not afford to keep them. There would be other animals on the farm as well. I remember Dad raising a pig and butchering it in the fall. This too was a painful time for me. There would be a few hens and lots of fresh eggs. Aggie would stay with us for a few years after this and, in fact, moved with us to our home on Fraser hill.

There were a few deer around, and once in a while, one would end up in our cold room. (In the winter, every room was cold.) My brother Keith would often say it was so cold, there was frost on the lampshade.

18

On one occasion, there were sheep on our land that were not supposed to be there. My brother Stewart chased them away one evening, but one old sheep was reluctant to leave. He ran after her in several directions until she finally followed the old path into the woods. The next morning when my brothers and sisters were going down the path to school, they found the poor old sheep dead on the trail. I guess she died of natural causes, or perhaps it was unnatural.

My father and I with the new Calves.

Buttermilk and Molasses Cookies

One of my first memories of traveling in a car was to a wonderful place called Sunny Brae in Pictou County. We had an aunt there. (She was actually my mother's aunt, but we all called her Aunt Martha.) She was one of the dearest people I ever met. She created a lasting impression on me.

Traveling from the Musquodoboit Valley to her home was about thirty-five to forty miles. In those years, that was a whole day's trip. To make a return trip in one day was unheard of. We would usually fill a car for the trip. It did not matter how many seats were in the car, just the number of people you could fit in. Being the smallest of my family, friends, and relatives, I would usually get to sit on someone else's knee or stand in the back with my face glued to the side window. This was an experience I will never forget. The long winding road was dusty or muddy depending on the weather. There were very few houses along the way but many trees. I remember traveling along looking out the side window at the trees that were just a few feet from the side of the vehicle. Tree after tree after tree. I loved it. From that day on, I have had a love for motor vehicles. My love for car rides was not without a little discomfort, however, as I was prone to car sickness from time to time. The joy of riding in a car overshadowed the illness, and I received a few of the old remedies that were sure to cure. I will not go into great detail, but I can assure you, the illness was better than most of the remedies that were thrust upon me.

There were many trips to Sunny Brae after that, and each one was very exciting. We would exit the vehicle and walk the few steps to the house, shaking the dust from our clothes. We would arrive unannounced most of the time. (I guess no one sent her an e-mail to let her know we were on the way.) She would always welcome us with laughter and big hugs. The smell of fresh biscuits, bread, pies, and cookies still float around in my little brain. The one thing that stands out the most was the big molasses cookies and buttermilk. As a young boy, I loved buttermilk and molasses cookies. These trips were a true joy for all of our family.

I am sure over my childhood years I had more than a few visits with my relatives, but Aunt Martha was the one who gave me the greatest thrill. It did not seem to matter how many came to visit or how long they stayed; she made us all feel special. Over the years, I have had the occasion to travel over most of Canada and many parts of the United States, but nothing has moved me like the smell of Aunt Martha's cooking.

It took me a long time to adjust after she passed away. She was a big influence on my life. Her smile and laughter were contagious, and many times when the going was tough, I thought of her and my problems seemed less important. She gave comfort and support to everyone in her community and many relatives from miles around. In our haste to accomplish things for ourselves, we would all be wise to slow down and remember the Aunt Marthas in the world. Take a moment once in a while to think of the many people that helped you along the way. I can't go back to the buttermilk and cookies, but I will always stop from time to time and savor the precious memories.

Don't wait too long to tell someone how much you love, how much you care, because when they're gone, no matter how much you shout, they will not hear. (Unknown)

Robert on Stewart Hill. Grandparents home far in the back.

Sister Thelma with our Cousin Cora Stewart Pearson. To the best
of my knowledge Cora was the last Stewart born on Stewart Hill.
Cora is the only one on this page who is still living.

Sister Frances Taylor Miller.

Malcolm MacLeod Taylor.

Mildred Jean Taylor.

Robert, Frances, Keith, and Stewart. Brother Dennis was at home.

Hard to Say Farewell

While this book is about boys for the most part, I want to make it clear that my sisters were equally important to our family. My three sisters were so different. Each had their own characteristics. They did not look alike, act alike, or live a lifestyle that was common to each other. They did, however, have strong family ties.

When Mildred was quite young, she had her own version of the nursery rhyme "Rain, Rain Go Away." Her version was, "Rain, rain go away, come again someday else." She was teased about this for a long time. She was one of a kind.

Thelma was born to laugh and enjoy life. She had more health problems than the rest of us, but she never complained. We had a lot of fun times together when she was with us, and I never heard her complain.

Frances was the team leader. In her motherly fashion, she took care of everyone in her sight. She was a blessing to our whole family. Her work never ended until she decided it was time to go.

Stewart Hill Acreage

I would like to mention a project that has had a tremendous impact on many members of the Stewart family. In 1975, my uncle Byron Stewart put together a plan to purchase property on Stewart hill. It was the start of a great campsite that is now one of the finest family campsites around. I will mention a few of the people who were also involved. Aside from Byron Stewart, there was Verna Stewart Sanford, Olla Stewart MacInnis, Erma Stewart MacDonald, Bruce Stewart, Ivan Stewart, Boyde Stewart, Peggy Stewart Sanford, Martha Stewart Dorey, and Michael Stewart.

The list of hardworking people continued to grow, and a company was formed. Shares were offered. They decided to have a family reunion every five years, and the numbers continued to grow. I am not sure what their record attendance has been at these events, but at least one had 450. It has been a true success story, and I expect it will continue for a long time.

I wanted to touch on this subject not because of the statistical side but because of the emotional rewards so many people have enjoyed over the years. I was born a short distance from the Stewart hill acreage site of today. From our house, I could look out over the property that is now a beautiful campsite. My mother would have been so proud of her brothers and sisters and all her nieces and nephews for their work in making this all happen. I make it a point to attend the reunions and always come away from there with so much enthusiasm.

Thanks so much to all the people who have given their time and effort to this very special cause. I know these events don't just happen. I also know that planning these events can create a lot of pressure and perhaps an argument or two along the way. The positive results, however, have been shown over and over again.

Another place dear to my heart was the old sugar shack that provided great maple products. The shack itself was situated in a large stand of maple trees just off the Stewart hill road. It was quite near the line between Colchester and Halifax counties. I remember several trips we visited and watched my uncles work around the old shack. The ones that impressed me the most were my mother's brothers Bryden, Elmer, and Byron. I would be willing to bet that the last few years they worked there together were the best of their lives. They worked hard, but they had time to entertain us and cuss each other. There was pipe tobacco and chewing tobacco on the go, and I am sure that maple products were not the only liquids consumed. For some reason, I always felt that their maple products were better than any other I had tasted. Perhaps it was the family connection.

There is another story that took place on Stewart hill around the time I was born. My grandfather Stewart had been quite ill and was confined to his bed. My father, who thought a lot of his father-in-law, made it a point to visit him as often as he could. When Grandfather was still up and about, he would often invite my dad to accompany him to the horse barn. There would always be a bottle of brandy in the oat bin for medicinal purposes. It seemed there were several ailments that would occur from time to time, and brandy was the only cure.

On one of Father's visits, he found Grandfather in his bed and speaking quite low. He said, "Clifford, would you go out to the horse barn and fetch me a sip of brandy?" Just a second or two before this, my grandmother came into the room and heard his request. She said to Father, "Oh, Clifford, the poor man is delirious. He never had a drink in his life.." Father then went to the barn and retrieved the bottle of brandy. My father was a very kind and thoughtful man and placed his father-in-law's request above any repercussions that may have taken place later on. He gave Grandfather a sip of brandy. I am not sure how long Grandfather lived after that, but I think it would be safe to say his time on earth was extended as a result of his special medicine that day. I never knew my grandfather, but my older siblings told me he sometimes had a stern look on his face but a cute little twinkle in his eyes. Sounds like someone I would have loved.

The Days on Fraser Hill

The move from Stewart hill to Fraser hill was rather a question mark to me. I did not realize the need, but on the other hand, I did not mind. To a young boy, it was not a big change. I don't know what prompted the move, but I would soon find a few new friends and be off to school in the fall. The old house was in a beautiful location. It was on a hill, of course, and the view from there was a treat for anyone. The house had been a grand abode in the years before, but needed a lot of work when we moved in.

The other buildings on the property were also in need of repair. After a lot of cleaning and several repairs, it became our new home, and we soon got attached to the big house on the hill. Our oldest brother Stewart had joined the navy by this time and was off to sail the seas. Our oldest sister Frances became our second mother and tried to keep us in line and comfortable. It must have been a hard time for her and my father, but I never heard them complain.

Shortly after we arrived there, Frances had a slight mishap at the old well outside. She had gone out for water. The well had a crib around it, and the bucket was tied to one of the boards. When she dropped the bucket down the well to fill it, the rope somehow became untied and the bucket fell into the well and floated on top of the water. The water was down several feet from the crib. She was worried our father would be upset with her, so she decided to crawl down the well and get the old bucket. As you can readily understand, these old wells were not in the best of shape. She managed to go down and retrieve the bucket and get out without a hitch. When Father came home from work, she told him what had happened. At first, he was upset with her for going down the well and then told her she was worth far more to him than any old water bucket. Frances was always a hard worker, and our family owes her a lot for the way she took over when our mother passed away. She has a large family of her own now, and they treat her with warm affection, which she surely deserves.

When we moved from Stewart hill, we brought Aggie and a few hens with us. We also had our dog Ranger. Aggie was the cow that I mentioned before. The hens were normal except for one, which was black. She was my pet, and I called her the black pullet. The dictionary calls a pullet a young hen. My pullet was a young hen all of her life. Shortly after we arrived, the black hen got caught in a snare that was probably set for stray cats. (We later scoured the area to make sure there were no more snares.) I was scared she had met her end in life, but Father came to our rescue and saved her for another day.

Our poor old Ranger did not fare so well. He was a beautiful fluffy white dog with one black ear. I do not know his breed, but he was a midsize dog with lots of hair. We all loved him. He was quite old when we moved and certainly not well enough to survive very long. One day, I saw my father take the dog with him back toward the woods. He had a gun with him, and I know he had tears in his eyes. (I say that now because I know the kind of man my father was.) He had to put our dog to rest. This may seem cruel and inhumane, but in those times, that was the normal procedure. That does not mean it was any easier to do then than it would be now. I was very sad for a long time, but we all find ways to deal with our losses.

It was on Fraser hill that I became closer to my brother Malcolm. He was six years my senior, but he was always good to me. He included me in a lot of things that most boys his age would never think of. If it was not a school day and he was going to visit friends or relatives, he would take me along. When the movies started in the old church hall on Monday evenings, he would always watch over me. I think I got into the movies for ten cents at that time. I remember those old movies like it was yesterday. It was in that old hall that I saw *King Kong, Gone with the Wind,* and many good old Western thrillers. When the horses ran across the screen, you could almost smell the dust in the air, and yes, the wagon wheels would be turning backward. (You have to be a senior to understand this.) As I got older, I went to these movies by myself and looked forward to the thrill of motion pictures.

One of the things I remember the most was the old swamp down over the hill from the house. Malcolm took me there, and the two of us dug ditches to help drain part of the swamp. We dug a small ditch and created a little water hole we called our lake. We had many good times there, and I treasure those days with my big brother. While we were still on Stewart hill, Malcolm, who was younger at the time, fell on a tin can and cut his knee quite bad. He ran to Mother for help. She comforted him and cleaned up the wound. While doing this, she asked him what had happened and he cried, "I was running much faster than I could and I fell on that old can."

Unfortunately, he passed away a few years ago, but I do have lots of good memories. The days on Fraser hill were days without our mother. Our father worked every day, and we were left to look out for ourselves. It was not easy, and I suppose there were days when we did not get three good meals a day. I don't really remember feeling any neglect on the part of my siblings, but there were times when I was very lonesome. There would be times especially in the summer when my brothers and sisters would go and leave me home alone. I know that each of them had a good reason. (Yeah right.) I survived and actually grew to enjoy my freedom.

A Ride in the Wood Truck

A short time after we became established on Fraser hill, Frances married Glen Miller, and they moved to Greenwood, a small community a couple of miles down the road. Glen had an old International truck that he used to make his living. I believe it would have been a two- or three-ton truck, which was normal for those years. He hauled gravel, logs, lumber, or anything that provided a few dollars. Around this time, he got an opportunity to haul a load of firewood to Truro. He had to go to a mill site up in Woodside or Chaplin, which was a few miles above Dean. Frances went along with him to help load the wood. This was all done by hand and would not be an easy task, especially for a very pregnant lady. They were expecting a new child any day. They got their wood on the truck and began their long haul to Truro. It would be about thirty-five miles. Frances sat in the cab with Glen, but apparently she was not very comfortable as she moved from side to side and appeared to be uneasy. When they arrived in town and dumped the load, she told Glenn she wanted to ride in the back as she felt she would be in less pain if she was standing up. Glen found a long piece of lumber for her to walk up onto the truck. She stood on the back of the truck and held on to the headboard. I am sure Glen was nervous and probably gave her a fast ride home. She held on to the headboard all the way home and let the wind blow free. The roads would not have been paved at that time and, of course, were rough. They managed to make it home to the Bill Stewart house, where they were living at the time. The long ride over the bad roads must have finalized the labor as their new son was born very soon afterward. Perhaps you could call this ride a form of induced labor. Frances gave birth to five more wonderful children after that, bringing her total family to seven.

My sister Frances passed away in October 2013. I miss her a lot as she was like a mother to me. She was not one to speak often, but when she did, it was always worth listening to. When Frances and her husband Glen came to visit in the summers, she and I would take the opportunity to watch baseball on television. She was an avid Toronto Blue Jays fan. On one of these occasions, Glen decided to join us and take in some of the game. After watching for a while, he exclaimed to Frances, "Why don't they throw that ball in a little slower? No wonder the batter can't hit it." Frances looked at him with one of her looks, and he decided he had seen enough of that crazy game and left us alone. She was also an avid Toronto Maple Leafs fan. When she passed away in October, the Leafs won their first three games of the season. Wow! She left us when they were undefeated.

Frances doing what she loved. Picking berries.

The old house on Fraser hill.

Tommy or Timmy

This is a story that very few people had ever heard. It is a funny story, yet sad because it happened when I was quite small and, except for me, the people involved are all gone. For about seven years, I lived on an old farm called Fraser hill in Upper Musquodoboit. This spot had a magnificent view of the valley and the community below. When we lived there, I don't think we realized just how beautiful it was, but many times since then, I have marveled at its splendor. My father rented the house on the farm as he was employed elsewhere and was not really a farmer.

Down the hill a short distance was another farm that was owned by William Fredericks. These people were all wonderful neighbors, and my brother Malcolm and I spent a lot of time there. It was at their home that I learned to play Monopoly. Malcolm, their son Howard, and I would play for hours. I was the squirt of the group, but they did not seem to mind and I learned fast. Mrs. Fredericks was a special lady and made sure we never left there hungry.

On one of my first visits there, Mr. Fredericks met me at the door and invited me in. He said, "Hi, Tommy, come on in." I looked at him and said my name was Robert. He smiled and told me I looked like a Tommy to him. I went inside and took off my cap. He looked at me again and said, "Hi, Timmy." Once again, I corrected him and thought he would get it right next time. He just laughed and said, "You know what, I think I will call you Tommy when you have your cap on and Timmy when you don't." From that day on, he called me Timmy. I have never shared that with many people, but I often think about it and smile. He was teasing me, but I know I must have impressed him in a small way or he would not have taken time out from his work to talk with me.

Mr. Fredericks gave me great joy by poking fun at me and calling me Timmy. I wish I could go back in the later years and thank him. It is sad when we miss an opportunity to tell others how we feel and then realize later it is too late. It reminds me of something I read many years ago: We grow too soon old and too late smart. I have often thought of these words when I realize I should have done something sooner.

I visited there once a week to deliver the *Standard*. (This was a weekly paper that a few people in the community received, and I was the local delivery boy.) I had eleven customers, and I got two cents for each customer. I had to walk over two miles and received twenty-two cents. I enjoyed the opportunity and liked meeting the nice people in the community. I always looked forward to seeing Mr. and Mrs. Fredericks as they were always nice to our family.

The Borrowed Tractor

Over the course of several years, I believe most boys will do something that is not quite legal. I must admit I did something just like that when I was about ten years old. We were living on Fraser hill at the time, and it was haying time on the old farm. The Burris family from farther up the road had rented the fields around the old house we lived in. They had just bought a beautiful Massey-Harris tractor that year. It was called a Pony. I loved that tractor! I watched it while they drove it all over the farm, raking hay and doing other chores as well. I wanted to have a ride on that tractor so bad, but I was too scared to ask.

One day at lunchtime, I went outside and saw that the men were leaving for lunch, and I knew they would be gone for a short time. I watched as they drove down the long lane and headed up the road through the village. When they were out of sight, I ran and jumped up on that beautiful red tractor. I thought I was in heaven. As I was sitting on the seat and playing with the steering wheel, I noticed that the keys were still in the ignition. I had never been around motorized equipment that often, but there is something in a young boy's brain that propels him when he comes in contact with any machines. Especially a Massey-Harris Pony tractor.

I looked at all the levers and pedals and soon realized what I would have to do to get this treasure started. The tractor was on level ground, and I decided to start it up. My legs were a little short, but I did manage to get the clutch in and the motor running. I could see the letter *R* on the transmission and pulled the lever back. I eased the clutch out, and the little tractor moved backward. I took a mental picture so I would remember exactly where it had been when I got it rolling first. I shifted gears and went back and forth a few times, then decided I had better leave it alone. I don't think I ever told a single person about this until now. Could I still be charged? I hope not. I guess if no one knew it was missing, then it was not stolen.

That was the start of a little love affair with Pony tractors. I never forgot that tractor, and in later years, I bought one and restored it to its original state. It was my pride and joy for a few years. I should also mention another thing about this neat little tractor. When I first got it, I used it a lot at our woodlot. It worked fine, and I loved driving it through the woods and mud. After I finished the restoration, I was afraid to take it into the woods for fear of scratching it. Then one day, a gentleman came along and offered me far more than it was worth. I decided to sell it to him and off it went. I still miss it, and perhaps one day I will have another. Some men are like that, and I am proud to say I am one of them.

My 1948 Massey Harris Pony Tractor Restored in 2001.

Early Days at Henry School

I wanted to tell this story because it was something that was on my mind for several years. I started school in the early forties, in Upper Musquodoboit. It was a two-room school. In those days, a school would be built in an area that was referred to as a section. The section I first attended was Henry section, thus it was called Henry School. I have mixed feelings about my time there; however, I do remember the good times. One thing that really stayed with me was a special teacher I had. Her name was Ruth Durning. She was my teacher for two years, grades one and two. She was a good teacher who helped us without any harsh words or reprimands.

She came to school one morning during the second year looking very sad and without her usual bubbly smile. It was only a short time before she broke down and cried before the class. None of us knew what had happened. We just knew something was wrong. She soon got back on track and went on like nothing ever happened. This bothered me for a long time. It was sad for me to see my teacher cry. By this time in my life, I had cried often, but I did not want her to cry. Many years later, I became acquainted with her brother and we talked about this incident. He was not aware of this, but he suggested I should go see her. I had thought of it many times before but never found the time to go. Then one day, I decided I would go. At this time, she was in a home for special care. We talked about school and the day she cried. She was so pleased to tell me all about it after about fifty-five years. She was also happy that one of her students remembered her after such a long time.

Some of the older boys in class were not paying attention like she thought they should and were not obeying her. Frustration got to her and she cried. When I was listening to her tell me about that day a long time ago, I wanted to find the culprits and give them a lesson in appreciation.

Sometimes a few kind words will heal a lot of pain. On the day I visited with her, I think we helped each other. She passed away shortly after that. I was saddened, but I am glad I got to see her when I did. She was one of the many great teachers we had in our schools.

Most of the exciting events at this school were carried on outside the school doors. These were not necessarily educational but I feel quite certain they were needed in order for a young boy to mature. In the winter, we would play in the snow and coast as much as we could. At the back of the schoolhouse, there was a nice hill to coast on. Sleds were not always available, but one year we hit gold. There had been a little canteen on the opposite side of the road. I am not sure who owned it, but it was no longer in use. On the outside of this little building, there were several pop signs of varying sizes. They were metal with a coat of enamel. We removed these and turned them into the best sleds you could ever imagine. Some of the signs were quite long and could accommodate several children. We had to bend them just slightly at one end to prevent them from digging into the snow. The smaller signs were used by individuals and became somewhat like the flying saucers we see today. There was a concern for safety sometimes as the edges were quite sharp. I think they were only used for a short time, but they were fast. At today's auctions, those old signs would be worth a small fortune.

When the weather started to warm up in the spring, it was off to play ball. This was all done at recess and lunchtime. I loved to play ball and joined in whenever I could. Some of the bigger boys would push us around, but we persevered and they let us play. There was a good field beside the school that made a great place to play. On one of the days we were playing, one of the boys started to act up a little. He was not showing any interest in playing ball but was annoying the rest of us. At this point, one of the bigger boys told him to get off the field. He decided to do so, but as he was leaving, he took the only bat we had and ran home with it. It was only lunch break, but he went home and stayed until the next day. When he came to school the next morning, he had the bat and assumed things would then be back to normal. Not so. My brother Mac was the first to accost him. They had words and then they wrestled for a short while. Finally, Mac got the best of the other boy and was sitting on his chest in the schoolyard. The other boy shouted, "Please don't hit me, Mac. I will give you an apple." Everyone laughed, and the whole event was soon history. In those days, almost every boy in school had a jackknife in his pocket, but they would never think about using it in a situation like this. They were used for whittling, sharpening your pencils, making whistles, cleaning fish, or perhaps cutting a little piece of tobacco off your granddad's plug when he was not looking.

I have many thoughts about that old school and drive by the old location quite often. One day, as we were leaving school, we noticed a huge black cloud across the road from the schoolyard. It seemed to be getting closer to the ground as we watched it. In the field just off the road, there were several piles of lumber that were stuck there to dry before they were loaded on the train. There were five or six of us leaving the school for home that day. We were the youngest ones at the school, and we always got out of school first. I don't remember being afraid, but the dark cloud came even closer and we could hear the wind as it seemed to intensify. As we walked down the road away from the lumber piles, we heard a funny sound. As we turned around to look again, there were pieces of lumber being lifted off the piles. None of us realized just what was happening, but it must have been a small tornado. When we told others farther along the road, they did not believe what we were telling them. It was not normal for anything like this to happen in our little village, but it did on this day. I hope someone who was at the school that windy day will remember that storm and corroborate my story. The only damage we found the next day was lumber scattered around the field. Some would later accuse the boys in the school for doing this, but we knew the truth. The school is gone now, and all that is left is the land, which is overgrown with weeds. My mother went to school there, and so did my brothers and sisters.

Walking to and from school was a difficult task during the winter months. Going to school was not too bad as some of my older siblings would go with me. Coming home was the problem as I had to walk by myself, and quite often the snow would cover our trail. We used a shortcut through the farm pastures as travel by the road was quite a bit farther. I got out of school early as I was the youngest of our family. There were many days that I walked through deep blowing snow and quite often was afraid I would get lost. I never told anyone because I did not think I was much of a young man if I was afraid.

This was normal for a country school in those days. Many others suffered the same feelings. If it was a school day, you went to school. Who would ever let their children stay home because of a little snow? I am not saying this was right. I am saying that is the way it was. When I did get home I was the only one there so I would start a little fire and then go out and play around in the snow. It was so much fun playing in the snow as opposed to walking to or from school.

39

Fourth Row:
1 Edith Stewart Redmond
2 Bessie Stewart Chaplin
3 Nellie Barnett Stewart
4 Roxie Fraser
5 Ernst Barnett
6 Nellie Archibald Ross
7 Gladys Archibald Andrews
8 Eben Holman
9 Mary McCurdy Barris Teacher
10 Melville Stewart

Third Row:
11 Alexander (Sandy) Parker
12 Melissa Fraser Ellebel
13 Lydia Harry Fredericks
14 Augusta Stewart Redmond
15 Laura Redmond Miller
16 Florence Archibald MacCarthy
17 Geraldine Kirk
18 Lizzie Farrell Logan Huton
19 Jean Archibald Durfnick
20 Almira Stewart Kene

Second Row:
21 Burnham Stewart
22 Annie McCurnigh
23 Helen Henry Leslie
24 Emma Farrell Filmore
25 Alice Archibald MacMillen
26 George Robert Burris
27 Clarence Stewart
28 Ernest Stewart
29 Elsie Stewart Hutchinson
30 Jean Stewart Taylor

First Row:
31 Stanley Farrell
32 Lillian Henry Johnson
33 Ralph McCurnigh

Please note. The placement of names and spelling may not be totally correct.

Stewart Taylor, Doug Deale, Tom Pinco, Stewart Hill.

Malcolm, Keith and Robert Taylor.

The Christmas Season

I don't remember much about Christmas in my early years, but one or two things come to mind. When we lived on Stewart hill, my brother Stewart made us our very own Christmas lights for the tree. Electricity was not abundant in the area at the time; however, our father had purchased a large battery and generator that was driven by a small gas engine. He had one or two lights in the house for personal use but never on a tree. We had a few Christmas ornaments that were round glass balls with horizontal painted stripes. They were quite common, and a few can still be seen around the older homes. He placed small flashlight bulbs inside a few of these and wired them. These lights may not have been all that bright, but to me, they were brighter and far more fascinating than the lights I would see many years later in New York City.

I was older when we moved to Fraser hill and have more memories. We loved to go down to the local general store during the Christmas season as they always had more exciting things in stock. What a treat to go in and see so many toys and all kinds of candy. By this time, our mother had passed away and our father was our only parent. We knew that our father could not afford most of these things, but he always found a way to purchase a few things we were not used to having. It was such a treat to have a few grapes, an orange, and sometimes a banana. There would be animal candy, ribbon candy, and sometimes special popcorn. All of these things were very special. Today, most of us take all of these things for granted.

One Christmas eve, I told my father I was going to run outside first thing Christmas Day to see Santa's tracks in the snow on the roof. Alas, when Christmas morning came, I was so excited I forgot all about it. By the next day, the snow had all melted and I could not see the tracks. We did not get a lot of toys and the treats were few, but we were so close to each other.

It was always exciting when we had our school Christmas concerts. We got to go to the big church hall and sing carols. If we were real lucky, our parents—in my case, older siblings—would come to see us. In those days, it was always a Merry Christmas theme.

Where have we gone wrong?

In later years, after our own children were born, Christmas took on a whole new meaning. We always tried to put their wishes first and provide for them the best we could. Those years were so much fun. The children would get so excited, along with their parents. Then came the grandchildren and the joy grew even more. When I think back to those days, I realize it was not always the gifts we got or the good food we had; it was the special days of Christmas that made us all so excited.

People who do not celebrate Christmas are missing out on a very special occasion. I don't pretend to be the most religious person on earth; however, I do believe there is something magical about Christmas. It is not about money and gifts. It is about how people come alive. We talk to people we don't even know. We think of our friends more at Christmastime. We dream about things we want to say and do for others. It is in the air, and it is a blessing no matter where you are. I firmly believe there is a power much stronger than any of us can understand that spreads this magic. I have decided to cling to this feeling of magic because it can work for everyone. I do not understand why anyone would try to hide Christmas like our politicians do. If ever there was a time to shout Merry Christmas, this and every year would be a good time to do so.

The Move to the Valley

After being born on Stewart hill then spending a few years on Fraser hill, I moved down into the Musquodoboit Valley. It was a short distance from my previous location, but I was not happy with the change. This was a very troubled time in my life for several reasons, all of which became ironed out over a short period of time. I will do my best to explain my hardship. After my mother died, we all had difficult times. I am sure each of my siblings and my father suffered for their own special reasons. I can't begin to answer for them, but I can relate some of my reasons for dismay. After several years without my mother, my father decided it was time to get married again. This was not a bad plan on my father's part, but it broke my heart. I did not want him to give up time with me in order to spend time with a lady I did not know.

My siblings were all getting older and more and more independent. Some of them married and/or moved away. All of them except me were old enough to make their own decisions. I did not have a choice. I had to move to another location about a mile from the old house we were living in. I had to go to another school, a newer house, and live with a new stepmother. I was ten years old. It was several months before I started to adjust. I cried at night, but I would never let anyone else know. I was determined to find a way to overcome my sadness without showing any signs of tears.

Shortly after I started school in the Hutchinson section, I started to feel much better. I met so many new and wonderful friends. I soon got to know my new stepmother, and we got along just fine. I grew very attached to her and learned so much from her. Shortly after this, she had a new baby boy. I had a baby brother Dennis. He was a joy to me.

I also found that the new house I lived in was so convenient. I had neighbors all around, and I found a new circle of friends. I still see a few of these friends from time to time. We always reminisce about some of the old times and share some laughter.

About the time we left Fraser hill to move to the new house, my brother Mac asked brother Keith if he could borrow his old bicycle. It was not the best bike in the world, and it was in rough shape. I guess Keith decided to let him have it even though he was not sure what Mac had in mind. (I found out later that Mac did not have permission to take the bike.) As it turned out, Mac was planning a trip to Wittenburg, Nova Scotia, which was about twenty miles away. He wanted to visit some of our cousins there as well as our grandparents. I don't think he told us how long he was staying. He just jumped on the old bike and off he went. After about a week, he decided to return home. He needed some money, so he sold Keith's bicycle and hitchhiked back to Upper Musquodoboit. I don't suppose he got a very warm welcome from his older brother. This was a long time ago, but I think he sold the bike for $2.

My home was situated about seventy-five feet from the railroad track. It was the Upper Musquodoboit to Dartmouth Railroad. The train left

Upper Musquodoboit early in the morning and made the round trip to and from Dartmouth, arriving back in the early evening.

To a young boy, there were not many things in life more exciting than that old train. When it passed our house, it would rattle the dishes in the cupboard. You could look out our kitchen window right into the cab of the train as it went by. The engineer or fireman would almost always wave as they passed. This was always a custom in our area and I suppose all along the many miles they traveled. There were train stations every few miles along the track. The larger villages would have a full-time station agent, and the smaller villages would have a small unmanned station. There is a museum depicting the old train in Musquodoboit Harbour. There you can see much more detailed information.

To most people, the train was a very large part of life in our community. It provided employment for several people, transporting goods to and from the area. Lumber, pulpwood, and limestone would be three of the biggest items shipped out the valley. There were a lot of days I would go down to the station yard on my way home from school just to watch the men loading the boxcars. There were no mechanical loaders in those days, just human power. It was fun to watch the big trucks loaded with pulpwood roll in and empty their wood into the boxcars. Each truck owner or driver would have at least one other man with them. They were referred to as strikers. There were a few of these men I knew by name. George Dean (later to become my father-in-law) and perhaps Diddy Dean would be one truck driver and striker, George Fraser and Percy Kent another. At that time, one of my favorites was Ted Sponagle and his striker Arnold Gale. Ted would always talk to us and blow the horn when he was passing us. This was always a big thrill to a small boy. The above-mentioned people are all gone now, just as the train and all the stations except for one, and that is now the museum in Musquodoboit Harbour.

It was hard work. They loaded their trucks, unloaded the wood into the boxcar, and then went inside and piled it up again. I think they hauled about four cords per load and probably hauled about four loads a day, depending on the distance they had to travel and conditions at the time.

Limestone was another product that took up several railcars every day. This was a very dusty job, so we did not linger long. I always felt sorry for the men that worked in that area. On the return trip from

Dartmouth, there would be a wide variety of freight that would be dispersed to stations along the route.

As a young boy, I was not too concerned about the business part of the railroad. I was just in awe of the size of the train and the sound of the old steam engine. I would love to go back to my old home place someday and be able to see the train coming up the track. The steam would be gushing out the sides, and the steam whistle would be blowing for the crossings. If there were children anywhere near, the engineer would even give them a little shot of the whistle too. I remember on several occasions we would hide under one of the train bridges as it went over us. This was an experience I will never forget. The rumble of the big engine and cars going over us would make us tremble as the steam and coal smoke would mix and fall down around us. The bridge would be about six feet above us when it passed over. We could feel the ground around us shake as the mighty iron horse rolled over. It was just as well our parents did not know what we were doing at the time. It was always nice to watch the farm animals in the pastures when the train came up the track. It seemed like the younger animals were afraid of the big train and would run, but the older ones just watched. Sometimes the horses would run along the fences as the train went by. One would almost think they had been waiting for it to come along. Those days are gone, but the smell of the train smoke along with the sounds and the thrills will always be with us.

The train, along with the roundhouse a mile up the track, was a source of much joy for all of us boys and girls as well. We would spend countless hours just watching the crew as they filled the coal cars and shunted cars into place for the next trip out. It was a place to hang out as long as we did not bother the crew. Sometimes we would even get a short ride on one of the cars.

It was always a welcome sound when the train whistle would blow for a crossing several miles down the track on a quiet night. Even as a young boy, I was glad to see the train again and to see it rest at the station awaiting an early departure the next morning. When the diesel trains took over the trip to and from Dartmouth, a lot of the mystique left us. We missed the sound of the whistle and the smell of hot steam and coal smoke. Things change, but not always for the best.

The railroad was also a very convenient means of travel on foot. Many people walked the track because it was shorter than the road through the village. I was one of these people along with several of my friends. It was also closer to the old meadow where we spent so many hours fishing eels, skating in winter, and swimming nearby in the summer. I walked from my home to the stores near the train station and also to my sister's home on many occasions.

It was one of these trips that I learned a very lasting lesson about showing someone you care. I was on my return trip from my sister Thelma's home. I was alone that day, which was not totally uncommon in spite of the fact that I had several friends. I came upon a large patch of brown-eyed Susans very near the railroad track. They were so pretty with the late afternoon sun shining down on them. I picked a large bouquet and started off for home wondering if my stepmother would like them. When I arrived home and she saw the flowers, she started to cry. She gave me a big hug and said, "They are the nicest flowers I have ever seen. How did you know they were my favorite?" For several years after that, I would look again for them to give to her. I notice now they seem to be quite plentiful, but years ago, they were hard to find. I learned a very important lesson for sure that day. I picked the flowers that day on my own doing to take to my stepmother. I learned that my small effort that day filled her heart with joy. She mentioned the flowers many times after that. It is so easy to take a little time to make others feel better, and it will stay with them for a long time. To this day, as I see brown-eyed Susans, I think of my stepmother's tears of joy. It is amazing how such a small act of kindness can do so much, yet we miss so many opportunities to do just that.

It was that railroad track where I learned to walk the rails for hundreds of feet without falling. I could put my ear to the rails and listen for the train. It was also there that we could gather small stones for our slingshots. They were just the right size and almost as round as marbles. With them we could shoot straighter, but I still missed my target most of the time. Now I am glad I missed so many times.

When my sons were little boys, they had their opportunity to put pennies on the track just like I used to. After the train went by, they would rush out to find the pennies, which were very thin by this time. It was a treat for me to see them enjoy one of the things I had done as a child.

The rails have all been removed from the tracks now, and in a lot of places, it is hard to see where the tracks were laid. A little sadness creeps in when I think of our loss. Little did I know years ago when I played along the track that I would someday be writing about the fun we had and then the demise of the old Blueberry Express. I am not sure how official this name was, but we sure used it a lot around our community.

The following is a poem by my nephew, Douglas Miller, depicting the old train and the beautiful flowers that surrounded my parents' home.

I do fondly recall from my childhood day,
Would anxiously await to run and play.
By my grandfather's house and yard out back,
Always heading to explore near the railroad track.

The wildflowers, a bouquet would brighten any table,
The color and splendor like a storybook fable.
Dotting the trackside in a brilliant gold,
A pretty sight for any eye to behold.

Their petals would reach out as if to say,
Pick me first, I'll help brighten any day.
When once did sway from many a passing car,
Trains pulling limestone to places afar.

But the trains have all gone and never come back,
It is all quiet now by the railroad track.
The flowers still grow, their brilliance still shine,
Many a happy memory will always be mine.

(D. Miller, January 1986)

My First Bicycle

think I was eleven or twelve when I got my first bicycle. It was well used, but I loved it. It was not unusual to get used items of any kind in those days. At a very young age, we all learned to appreciate anything we received because we knew our parents went without in order for us to have a few things of our own. I took to that old bicycle like a duck to water. I did not have to be told that if I broke it, I fixed it. I soon became very good at patching tires, fixing chains, and numerous other mechanical failures. Most of my friends had bikes, so we made a lot of trips around the village. One of our favorite trips started up a long hill. Most of this hill was too steep to pedal as we were not blessed with several gears. Just one. We pushed up this long hill then traveled along an old road that was rough but fun to ride on. From this old trail, we crossed over to another old road that went downhill all the way to the main road again. This was the fun part. We rode free for almost a mile all downhill. What a thrill it was. The only safety items we had were the pants leg clips. Remember them? Helmets were not even thought of. Our old pants would be flapping in the wind and we would be frozen to the handle bars for dear life. Sometimes when we were on a rough part of the road, our teeth would chatter. It was fun, and we never suffered any major injuries.

There was another place we went to when it was nice and warm. There was a nice lake on the Sheet Harbour Road called Mill Lake. On the way to this lake, we had to go up a steep hill. We would have to push our bikes up that hill. About halfway up, there was an old lady who lived in a shack almost on the road. Her name was Kate Ogden. She was nice, but we were afraid of her. When we walked our bikes past her house, we always kept looking for her. If we saw her, we were real nice and polite.

When we came back, we were going downhill on our bikes so we would yell at her. She could swear like a trooper and she did. We all liked her and would never harm her. Even though I was afraid of her, I am sure she would never hurt us. Scare us yes, but hurt us no.

Fishing for Eels

There were times during the summer when we would get bored with the normal things we were doing and set out on a new adventure. I don't think we ever looked forward to going back to school; we just needed something else to expand the vast knowledge in a young boy's mind. One of these adventures was fishing for eels in the Musquodoboit River. I am not sure of the exact time in August nor the size of the crew we had. I will stick to first names to protect the identity of the boys involved. On most of these adventures, there would be three to five boys—Elliot, Ronnie, Kevin, Garry, Frank, and Robert. On some occasions, there would be others, but this was the core of the "gang." I use the word *gang* in a lighthearted manner because we were just a group of harmless boys. We probably preferred to be called a gang, but we were just boys. Once in a long time I will meet one of these boys and we will reminisce about the fun we had on our many excursions.

On one particular eel-fishing trip, we departed on an old raft we had built and repaired many times. It was always fun to get the old craft out on the water and pretend we were Tom Sawyer. We were not on the Mississippi, but we were having fun. The raft was old and not designed for speed or rough water. It would take us several hours just to do the necessary repairs. Rope was always scarce, so quite often we would use binder twine, which was always around for our taking. Some of the logs were so badly waterlogged that they would barely stay above water. It was not an easy task, but the fun we expected would far outweigh our efforts.

The dress for these occasions was very simple—long pants rolled up to just below the knees, a light shirt, and an old pair of sneakers. Come to think of it, that was the dress for almost every activity we would take part in all summer.

The best spot for catching eels was upstream about a quarter of a mile. The current was not swift because of the flat land in that area. The water ran very slow. We traveled from our local swimming hole where the raft was usually tied up. We poled along, using long peeled poles to propel us on our journey.

The area we were seeking was in the old meadow where the river took many turns. The water was quite deep, but the banks of the river were not far apart. For some reason, it was great for eels. Now I should explain we had no intention of keeping any of the eels as they were never eaten in our community as far as I know. It was an adventure. The journey itself was the most fun. We would slowly wind our way along the flowing river and feel the hot August sun on our bodies. Once in a while, our poles would stick in the mud at the river bottom. When this happened, one of the other boys would try to speed the raft up with their poles. In doing so, it would cause you to go off balance and quite often fall in the black water. It happened quite often. It was always a desperate time to get back on board. Laughter from the raft could be heard for miles around, I am sure. There was always a fear that while you were in the water, the biggest eel would be there to chew on your legs.

Once we had made our way to the best fishing area, we would anchor the craft and begin to fish. This was a very simple exercise. Take a fishing pole, lots of hooks, a pair of old gloves, a good knife, and lots of bait (worms). The eels were very easy to catch. Just bait your hook and toss the line into the water. They would take right away. The process was very straightforward. Haul the eel in, put on your old gloves, hold the eel long enough to get the hook out or cut the line, then throw the thing as far back in the meadow grass as you possibly could. In doing this, you could be sure the birds would get them before they returned to the water. Now there would be a great variance in the number we caught, depending on the person you talk to. I will tell you the numbers were not real high, simply because it was great fun for a short time and then we had other serious things to do that day.

The return trip down the river was always so much easier, as you could gently guide the craft along as you talked to your mates and argue about who caught the most or the biggest. There would be time to laugh and tease each other and perhaps make plans for a big game of kick the can later on that evening. I am not sure how many times we did this, but I do know that it is something I will always remember. I think we would have been somewhere between ten and fourteen years old at the time. As I think back, I wonder if our parents knew where we were. I am sure it was a constant worry for them, but we were young boys out having a great day without drugs or alcohol.

We all had our chores to do at home before we could set out on one of our ventures. I grew up in a farming area, but my parents did not live on a farm. I always had work to do at home, but it seemed like the farm boys had much more to do than I did. When my work was done, or I thought it was done to the best of my limited ability, I would always be around to help the farm boys with their chores. In doing so, it gave us more daylight hours for our much-needed bonding.

I go back along that river many times on my way through the Musquodoboit Valley, and I am always reminded of the great times we had there. The old meadows through which the river flowed provided lots of fun for us year-round. In the winter, the meadow would often flood and then freeze, giving us a natural skating area. You will hear more about this in other parts of the book.

We can't go back to those days, but remembering them is a blessing. I firmly believe the early days in our lives dictate the years to follow. We were not given much beyond the absolute necessities. I don't remember ever asking for much; there was never a reason to do so. Given the bare minimum, we did just fine. I always had dreams of better things ahead in life, but I also realized that enjoying the things we had was an integral part of growing up.

I still enjoy the trips through the Musquodoboit Valley and often think of the many adventures we experienced when we were still growing boys. Some of those friends who were on board for those great adventures are far away now, but I am sure they remember the great times we had. I, for one, can still feel the black mud in my old sneakers and the time I would have to clean them before I got home.

In dry dock after the fishing trip on the Musquodoboit River.

The Garden Hose

The alarm was ringing like the siren on an ambulance. It was seven o'clock in the morning, and I had a job to go to. I was already pressed for time as I rushed to get my clothes on for this big construction job. I think I was thirteen years old, and this was to be a paying job. I had just finished school for the year and was asked by a neighbor if I would help pour cement for his new house. I agreed, of course, as I had exciting things to do that summer, and the money would give me a slight advantage over the poor guys who did not have a job. Now let me explain. Every boy in our area had plenty of work to do that summer; however, they would not all get paid.

As I left my parents' house that fine sunny morning, I could almost feel the coins jingling in my pocket. I was about to take on a job I knew nothing about, yet I was confident I would learn fast, make a lot of money, and then seek other employment. My new job was to wheel cement up a few planks and dump it into the forms. How difficult could this be? I would soon learn that this was not easy in any way, shape, or form. I did not realize this at the time, but this was to be more of a learning experience than a paying job. It was more like volunteering to do something just for the knowledge. There were other young boys there as well, and we decided to do our best and hope the owner would be so happy he would be sure to pay us.

In those days, there were no cement trucks driving up full of ready mixed cement. It was all done on the site by hand. The gravel, sand, and powdered cement were all blended with the correct amount of water in an old steel drum that was turned with a gas engine. This in turn was dumped into a wheelbarrow and wheeled up the plank and into the forms. The water came from a small pump also run by a gas engine and pumped into a huge steel barrel.

There were several young men helping that day and at least one little guy too young to work. His name was Darrel. He was a curious little fellow and walked around looking at everything he could see. After a short time, he found the garden hose that was used to fill the big water barrel. The hose ran from the brook that was several feet away. The pump used that day was near the brook as well. The pump was running steady, and the barrel would be overflowing most of the time.

Darrel was having a great time with the hose and playing in the water. His father, who was working there as well, saw Darrel and decided to have some fun with the little fellow. He picked up the hose and crimped it in his hand, careful not to let the little guy know what he was doing. When the water stopped flowing, Darrel was surprised and looked around to see if anyone knew what he had done. His father shouted at him, "Darrel, what have you done to the hose?" Darrel said he thought he broke something. His father told him the only thing he could do now was to suck on the hose as hard as he could and perhaps that would start the water flow again.

Darrel did just that, and his father released his grip on the hose. The little fellow had the hose in his mouth when the full force of the water hit him. At first, the water almost choked him and tears came to his eyes. Later, when he realized he had fixed it, he started to smile. Most of us were taking a break at this time to watch the show. Just a few minutes later, he told his dad he was going to go home. He never ventured back all day.

We continued on with our construction job and finished about suppertime. It was a hard day's work, and it certainly was a learning experience. I also learned that not all people live up to their commitment. We went home unpaid and tired.

Cartoon by Kendall S. Taylor.

Kick the Can: Let the Games Begin

We played many games in our area, and most of them required very few props. We played tag, ante over, hide-and-seek, I spy, may I, and many more. There was also softball, a little ground hockey, and other team sports.

The one game that stands out most in my mind was kick the can. I suppose there are many versions of this game, but I will give you the game according to Robert. The rules were quite simple: First you had to find a suitable can. Our preference was an apple juice can. I think they were one-quart cans or perhaps a little smaller. It was always best to have several cans available as they had a very short life span. This was due to the beating that was thrust upon them. It was always nice to have several people playing the game; however, any number between four and twelve would fit the bill. In our area, we had eight or ten average. This could surprise you, but girls were not only allowed, they were encouraged to take part.

The rules were similar to the regular game of tag but much more exciting. Once the can was found, it was placed in the right location; ours was placed in the Whitmans' driveway about fifteen feet from the house. I should explain that the Whitman home and small farm were ideal for our many games, Not just because of the location, but more importantly, because of the great people they were. The mother, father, and grandmother actually seemed to enjoy a group of children charging around their yard, laughing and creating havoc. If my memory serves me correctly, there were five children in the family at that time, and three of them would be taking an active part in the game. I am sure the two youngest would be close by. After the can was placed, we would pick our first leader or loser, depending on our personal thoughts. This was done by an elimination process. We used the one potato, two potato method.

There were many others, but this was our favorite. The newly chosen leader had to face a wall, close their eyes, and count to one hundred. While this was being done, all the others would run and hide. When the leader was finished, he or she would try to locate the others one at a time. This is where the fun started. When the leader located any of their prey, they were to come back to the station. Station was the site where the leader counted. They were to remain there until the game was finished unless this is the part where the leader has the most problems. Everyone caught must stay at the station until all others are caught. If one of them still in hiding manages to come out, run, and kick the can before the leader catches them, everyone is then free. If this happens, they all run and hide again. If the leader was successful and found all members of the group before any of them kicked the can, the first one caught would have to become the leader or loser.

The cycle could go on for a long time. The leader would have to locate the can, bring it back to its original site, and then attempt to find the others. I have had many opportunities to kick the can and also try to find all who were hiding and bring them back to the station. I cannot remember any game that was more fun. When you break from your hiding place and beat the leader to the can, it was such a feeling of exhilaration to kick that can and see it fly through the air and hopefully land several yards from its rightful location. Each time one of us got to kick the can, there would be loud shouts from the others that were freed from the station. On a still evening, I am sure the roar would be heard a mile away. Over the course of an evening, everyone would get at least one chance to kick the can. I don't think any of us ever tired of the feeling when our foot hit that can.

The world has changed so much since then. I am not complaining and I don't think we are headed in the wrong direction, but it would be great to have a giant playground where all these games could be reintroduced to our children.

Pure Black Earth

As soon as school was over for the year, our thoughts would turn to the old swimming hole by Carl Whitman's hay field. This was a small pool in the Musquodoboit River that we all thought was the greatest place to be during the warm summer months. It was a place to swim, a place to meet friends, and in some small way, a place to grow and learn.

We would spend hours and hours there when the weather was right. There was always room for anyone who felt like swimming. We would gather there as soon as we finished lunch and our usual chores. Change rooms were never an issue during those days. The girls and the boys each had their own little niche carved in the alder bushes. From time to time, I suppose some would wander from one to the other; however, I never felt the need to do so at a young age. There were screams from the girls from time to time as some brave young soul would wander in the wrong direction.

It was a simple chore to cut out a small square in the vast amount of alders along the river. We would find a secluded spot and cut a trail. We made sure the trail was zigzagged a bit to hide the view from the field. During the summer months, the bushes were in abundance so cover was always there. We had lots of branches to hang our clothes on while we swam.

I was never a real good swimmer, but I loved the water and could keep my head above the surface most of the time. Swimming was always a great pastime for us, and the many other activities associated with swimming were also a lot of fun.

For a short time during August, the lamprey eels would appear and make life a little uneasy. Many stories evolved about their habits and how they could devoir a small boy in seconds. As we grew older, we found they were just there as a natural thing to do and seemed to coexist quite well with humans. It was always fun to watch them build their nest or hole in the riverbed to spawn. They would drag rocks from the river bottom and create a circle with them. The circle would be about a three foot radius and would be about six to eight inches deep. They would be around for a couple of weeks and then they were gone. Our swimming would never be curtailed, but we watched them very closely. Someone told us once that they would be gone after the first thunderstorm. This was not true, as we checked many times after a storm and they were still there.

We could be found there any afternoon and some evenings, as long as the weather was favorable. I remember one evening we were helping Carl Whitman get in some of his last hay for the season. When we were finished, he asked us to join him in an evening swim. We thought that would be fun because it was very rare for an adult to join us. We told him we would run home and get our swimsuits. He laughed and told us not to worry it would just be the guys and swimsuits were not necessary. We were a little reluctant to show that part of our bodies that had never seen the sun; however, he convinced us to try it. We joined him in the swimming hole, and one of us kept a close watch to make sure the girls were not nearby. Oh, how we change as we get a little older. I always admired Mr. Whitman for joining us that evening. It was not until years later that I truly realized what a good friend he was to all of us. He always found a way to make us laugh, and he was like a big brother to us. He was not only kind to us, but he also treated us like we were older than we really were. To a young boy, there is nothing better than to be treated like an adult. Mr. Whitman has left us, but I will always remember him and the fun we had.

One year just shortly after we started the swimming season, one of the boys hit upon a great idea. On one side of the swimming hole was an old pasture. It was flat for the most part, but sloped toward the river very slightly. Under the sod, the soil was very fine and black. The plan was to cut the sod off in a straight line from the river back about twenty-five feet. We cleared the sod about four feet wide in a line that was perpendicular to the river. Our next chore was to carry water to pour over this nice black earth. After this was done, we had a water slide like you never saw before. We could run for several feet, hit the muddy part, and off we would go sliding right into the river. This was great fun for one and all, and we spent many happy hours taking a mud bath and a dip in the river just a split second later. If there was a flaw in this plan, it was in the maintenance. You see, it was in a pasture where cattle would graze from time to time. It was always very important to check the black earth for deposits before one took the first slide. One could not put a price tag on projects like this; it would be small, but the joy we got in return was priceless. I suppose the slide is long gone, and I am not sure if anyone ever swims there now. Times change and people move on, but the memories will always remain. It has been many years since I have visited the swimming hole, but on one occasion, I did visit when I was in the area. I was a lot older then, and the river looked so small. The important thing is the memories are everlasting.

The people we met there are now scattered for many miles, and some of them have left us for good. It was a great way to enjoy some of the simple things in life and learn from the experience. During the many exciting days at the old swimming hole, there was never a need for anything but fun and laughter.

During these times, we could always find little extra things to do as well. Almost everyone around us had a garden, so fruit and vegetables were abundant. We were not always welcome, but most of our neighbors were very tolerant. My favorite vegetable was cucumber, taken right off the vine. Carrots were great as well, and when we could find wild strawberries, we were very happy. Chokecherries were also good if you made sure they were ripe. They were usually in abundance so we could eat as many as we wanted. After a few of them, our mouths would get all twisted up inside from the juice. There were lots of apple trees in the area. We started eating them as soon as they formed on the branches of the trees. Green apples or red, we ate them whenever we could. If they were too hard to eat, we would throw them at each other.

Making Hay while the Sun Shines

I worked for a kind gentleman farmer for two summers. The first year, I was paid one dollar a day. It was well into the fall before I got paid, but it was money in my pocket. Early the next spring, I talked to my father and I told him I was going to ask the farmer to pay me two dollars a day that summer or I would not do it. My father thought I was asking too much, but he told the gentleman what I wanted. He agreed so I doubled my wages. I worked that year with new enthusiasm. I could not wait to get my money. When he came late in the summer to pay me, he announced that he could only pay half the money that day. He said he would get the rest as soon as he could. I never did get another cent from him. The good old farmer outsmarted the young boy.

Several years later, I was talking to another friend who was working on the farm next door at the same time. When I told him how much money I got paid, he started to laugh. He said he worked all summer and all he got was a live bantam rooster to take to the exhibition. He could put it on display, and this way, he would not have to pay to get in. I asked him what he did with the rooster after the exhibition was over, and he said he thought the rooster was still down there in one of the barns.

This reminds me of a quote I read a short while back, and I will share it with you.

It was on my fifth birthday that my father put his hand on my shoulder.

Remember, son, if you ever need a hand, you will find one on the end of your arm. (Sam Levenson)

A Brush with the Law

I remember the day well. It was in late August, and school would soon be starting. To a young boy, that was not a feeling of joy. I was with Elliot Whitman that day, and we were enjoying the last few days of freedom before we were ushered into the school and looked down upon by a stern teacher. We decided to have a bit of fun over by the old river bridge. This was a great place to hang out as the bridge provided all kinds enjoyment. We could fish there, swim, make our own little boats, and let them float around in the eddies under the bridge. Some days, there would be several boys and sometimes girls around as well. Because of our age at the time, we preferred to have just boys. On this day, there were just two of us.

As we sat on the riverbank and pondered our adventure for that day, we had no idea how big an adventure we were headed for. The sky was clear and the sun was hot, so we decided to just hang around there until an idea hit us. Soon we heard the sound of a car approaching. To our surprise, we also heard it slow to a crawl as it reached the old bridge. We turned to look and quickly noticed it was a police car. We were concerned as it was very rare to see a car there, let alone a police car. One of the officers got out of the car and shouted to us, "Hey, boys, come here and get in the car." He seemed to me to be ten feet tall and very mean looking. We crawled up the riverbank and did just what he told us. What else could we do? We were like two little mice in that big black car. We had no idea what would happen to us.

The two policemen started to question us right away. One said, "So you guys were out breaking windows last night." This was not a question. We looked at each other with fear in our eyes, but we both knew we did not break any windows the night before or any other time for that matter. The conversation continued with the two big policemen doing the talking. "We heard there were several windows broken in the school last night, did you fellows know that?" I think it was lucky for us we did not know this at the time. I think they saw the look of surprise along with the fear in our eyes.

"So you two boys did not do this?"

"No, sir, we did not even know there were windows broken." They kept us in the car for what seemed to us to be hours. I think it was only a few minutes. Without saying much more, they watched us very closely. I was too scared to say anything or look at my friend, but I was starting to get angry because we both had better things to do that day. We just did not yet have time to decide what it was going to be. After asking us if we had any idea who had broken the windows, they let us go. At that time, we did not know who it was, but we did find out a few days later. It was two other boys who will remain nameless.

We were not completely out of the woods yet, as we lived near the old bridge and our parents could see us. In those days, if a police car was in the area, everyone in the community would see it. We knew we would have to answer to our parents and they would be as tough as the two policemen. We decided to face the parents right away and we would give each other a full report later.

When I got home, I had to answer just as many questions as before, only this time I was not afraid. I told my parents just what had happened and that I was not involved in any window breaking at any time. I think I was convincing, but I am sure they must have wondered a bit about the whole thing. I was always one to believe that if you knew you were innocent, that was all that was needed. I have since learned that it is also nice to be able to prove it. In a few days, we were informed that the real culprits had confessed and we were finally off the hook.

Later on in life, I developed a strong sense of pride in the RCMP, and I still have that feeling. Even then, they were still just trying to do their job, but I am sure they did not know how close they were to having a big mess in the back of their car.

Fun Days on Clyde Hill

One of our favorite locations was Clyde hill. Over the years, I suppose the name has lost some of its luster; however, as a child, it was a great place to play, summer or winter. I am not sure where the name derived from, but I assume it was a place named after an older resident. It is a small hill situated in Upper Musquodoboit. It is across the road from the United Church and down slightly toward the Watson hill road.

It has not changed much over the years; however, a few houses have been removed and others built nearby. As children, it appeared like a giant anthill without any ants. It was steep, but not too high, excellent for coasting; and given the shape of it, one could coast on almost any part of the hill. It was close to the main road, but there was never any danger of reaching there from the hill unless you were dragging your sled.

There were many winter months when children from all parts of the village would gather there for hours. Walk uphill with a sled in tow. Coast downhill much faster. Repeat this exercise more times than we could count. Based on the speed going up versus the speed going down, we would spend less than 15 percent of our time actually coasting. In addition to this, we would do everything possible to make our sleds run faster, thus, in theory cutting our enjoyment time even more. Rather strange when you look at it like that, but it was all fun.

I have many fond memories of this hill and funny stories to go along with the experience. There was one winter season the sleds were scarce. (Perhaps Santa had to cut back on sleds that year.) We were forced to make do, and this was one of our strong points. My dad drew a picture of a sled he had made when he was a child. It was made out of old barrel staves. I began to look for a good barrel, that is, one not in use, yet still had a few staves on it. Word spread around there very quickly, and several of the boys were searching for barrels.

Once the staves were rid of any metal parts that may have been attached, it was time to polish the outer side of the staves. There were two staves needed for each sled. Most of the barrels we used were made of oak, which seemed to work the best. The finished product was very simple. Two staves placed about sixteen inches apart, two cross pieces on the ends, and a wide board for a seat.

If the construction was done properly and the staves were waxed properly, you would have a sled that would go like a scalded cat. This type of sled could be called the forerunner to the flying saucer. The speed was great, but they were rather hard to steer, causing many collisions on the hill. I am not sure what others called them, but we named them belly bumpers. Later on, we would all get a few store-bought sleds, but the old belly bumper provided us with the most laughs.

A few years later, one of my brothers was home on leave from the Canadian Air Force. He said he would like to go coasting while he was home. The next morning, we were awake early and off to Clyde hill. It had snowed overnight, and the hill was covered with new snow. There was not a track in the snow when we arrived, a great chance to play a trick on my brother.

There was one part of the hill that we had learned to steer clear of. Years before we were born, there was an old road that went across the hill about one-third of the way up. I think it was part of the old Guysborough Road that once ran from Halifax to Guysborough. When they built the road, they dug into the bank, and in one place, it left a cut into the upper side and a steep drop on the lower side of the hill. Most of the old road was leveled off over time, but this one place still remained.

Because it had snowed the night before, my brother did not know exactly where we were going to go down the hill. On this occasion, one of my friends had a nice new toboggan that would handle the four of us for the first trip. We pointed the toboggan toward the drop-off and suggested my brother should get on first up front. He agreed right away, making the joke almost too easy. We all got on, but the three youngest boys had no intention of going all the way down the hill. When the toboggan started to gather speed, we eased off the toboggan and left Mac all alone. Within seconds, he was airborne over the bank on the upper side of the old road. He dropped about four feet, hit the flat part of the road, and quickly shot out into the air once more, this time coming to rest in about eighteen inches of drifted snow. Mac was never one to hold back when he had something to say. He was very explicit that morning, and some of the words were not suitable for print in any book. I was quite proud of him other than his oratory on the evils of playing tricks on your brother. He did not mind the little surprise we gave him and continued to coast with us on the regular part of the hill.

My brother Malcolm MacLeod Taylor has gone from us now, and we all miss him very much. He had a harsh voice at times, but he had a heart of gold.

Clyde Hill in the Summer

Clyde Hill in the summer was always a treat when we broke from school for the Easter break. (In those days, it was an Easter break as opposed to the March break the students enjoy now.) Because it was an Easter break, we sometimes had weather warm enough to have a game of ball. There was a part of hill that was quite flat at the base and at the back. It was a nice spot for playing ball. There was never a lot of people around our community, but when word got around that there would be a ball game, people seemed to come from everywhere.

I remember several times in early spring we would gather there, boys and girls, to play ball and enjoy the warmer weather. Several years later, there was a nice golf course built in the same area. It was a nine-hole course, and number six hole was very near to our old ball field and was right at the base of Clyde Hill. Sad to say, the golf course has been abandoned and has weeds grown into it.

There are times when changes happen and we do not have control over the outcome. In that small area, I had the opportunity to play ball, coast, play golf, and also fished in the little brook. I walk by there on several occasions to hunt nearby. I am sure there were many generations of children who played on that same hill. On a few occasions, there were church services held on that same hill. Oh yes, it was a popular attraction.

I drive by there quite often and always look up to see the hill called Clyde. Perhaps one day I will see sled tracks again, and who knows, I might even have a coast.

There is another coasting story that should be told; however, it did not occur on Clyde hill. It all took place on the Watson hill road. The road ran from the main highway up a long hill and then down toward the Stewiacke Valley. The coasting we remember occurred on the Musquodoboit Valley side. Directly across from this road was the infamous Caribou gold mines road. The Watson hill road was not real steep, but it had a long gradual slope. Not all the roads were passable other than on foot. The portion we used was over a half mile from the main road to the only house on the hill. It was near the top. Motor vehicles could use this portion, but it was never a busy road.

Because of the gradual slope, coasting could not be done unless conditions were perfect. That is what made this hill so special. I am sure you have all experienced a time when everything came together. This is what happened one day when we got off the school bus and realized the snow conditions were just right. The previous night, it had rained, causing the snow to settle. Following the rain, it turned to freezing rain and then turned very cold. This created a very solid base of snow with the top frozen solid. Just prior to this, there had been trucks hauling down Watson hill and there were ruts in the road. We knew we were in for a great coast. We had to prepare for this and quickly put a plan together. Our initial plan was to build a long sled that would hold several people. We knew it was going to be a long slippery walk up the hill, and one sled was enough to handle. At the time, Elliott and I were the only ones involved. We found a long wide board that would serve the purpose. We found two hand sleds, one we fixed solid to one end of the board, the other we made to steer from left to right and vice versa. It was attached to the opposite end of the board, this being the front of our sled. We were very careful that both sleds were pointed in the same direction. This part of the plan all came about in a few minutes.

Our original plan was to gather a few together that night and have a coasting party. This all changed when Elliott came up with a fun idea. At the time, his father and another gentleman were cutting wood at the top of Watson hill. He suggested that since it was almost time for the two men to come down the hill, we should offer them a ride on our new sled. It seemed like a great idea, so the both of us started off up this long slippery hill. We found that the snow at the very edge of the road was not as slippery as the rest and eventually we got to the spot where the men were working. It was quitting time, and we asked them if they wanted a ride downhill. I knew Mr. Whitman would enjoy the ride because he was just a boy at heart. The other gentleman I was not so sure about. His name was Ira. He was hearing impaired and, because of this, could not speak a language that was easy to understand. I knew Ira well and liked him very much, but was not sure he would take advantage of our newest method of transportation. After a few encouraging words and hand gestures, they decided to take part. I don't remember how much gear they had, but I think they each had an old army bag over their shoulders. In these bags would be the remains of their lunch along with matches and other necessities.

I did not mention this before, but this road was straight from top to bottom. No need for any sharp turns. Once we were all on the sled, the fun began. One little nudge, and we were off. Elliot was steering and I was close behind him. The two men were close to the back of this long sled and soon became vulnerable. If we had been flying an aircraft, perhaps we would have considered weight distribution, but that did not occur to us at that particular time. The rear end of the sled started to swerve just slightly, this in part caused by the ruts in the hard snow. The driver looked back to see what the problem might be and in doing so created a problem that was worse than before but much more interesting. By this time, we were traveling at a fast rate of speed. Our craft was designed without brakes, so stopping was not one of our options. Ira was at the very back and lost his balance as the sled went into a slide. He rolled off and started his own slide down the hill. He was on his back and moving quite fast on the hard snow. I was hard-pressed to see all the action as I had to hang on. I did manage a quick look back and watched him come to rest at the side of the road. Mr. Whitman watched for a spot to get off where he would not suffer too much and walked back to see if Ira was okay. Elliott and I continued our trip down to a point where the road was flat and came to a halt.

We decided to walk up to meet the men, but when we approached, Ira made some gestures and loud noises. If it were to be translated, it would be something like this: "Gee, that was fun! Can we go again?" Perhaps he was not all that happy, but he laughed with us. I don't remember using that particular sled after that. It was a lot of fun, and no one got hurt. I can't help but think about all the work we did to build the sled, drag it up the hill for over a half mile, just for a little run down the hill that was over in less than five minutes. Mother Nature gave us the right conditions for that sled ride, and we took advantage of it. That

73

is life. Work hard for the things that are important at the time, and never forget the fun you had.

Hockey Days and Nights

From the first time I saw people playing hockey, I wanted to learn to skate and, of course, play the game. The first few years, I was lucky just to find an old pair of skates. Let me try to describe the first pair I had. They were called bob skates. They resembled a set of bobsleds. They had two blades or runners that were parallel to each other. They were made to fasten to regular boots. The ones I had were fastened with leather straps. I am not sure if they were handed down from one of my siblings or from another source, but they were not new for sure. When I tried to move on them, I found myself on my seat more than my feet.

The next skates were also well used. They were the normal-type skates of the day, and I had a great time with them. The upper part was leather, but very soft. When I put them on and tried to skate, my ankles would bend over and hit the surface. I say surface because I was usually a fair distance from the ice when I put them on. The lower part of the skate was metal, of course, and would quite often be loose. The boots were rivetted to the skate and over time would get loose. We would try to repair them, but this would only last for a short time. Sometimes the rivets would fall out completely, and we would replace them with some crude bolts we found wherever possible. For several years, I managed on skates in this condition.

During those years, I must have wished for new skates but that I don't remember. I was so happy with what I had, and I was enjoying life to the fullest when I had skates on. It was not until later years that I got my first pair of new skates. I was thrilled with them as they were from my three sons.

When I was about ten years old, some of the men in our community of Upper Musquodoboit got together and built a new outdoor rink. It was situated near the river, right in the center of the community. They

75

also built a rink house, installed lights, and placed boards around the ice surface. I was there as often as circumstances would allow. Sometimes I would just skate, and once in a while, I would get a hockey stick and pretend I was a superstar.

Most of the time, the younger boys would just stand around and watch the big boys play. We would hang around the sides of the boards with our skates on and ankles nearly touching the ground, pretending we were going to get a turn on the ice.

What a thrill it was to be able to go in the rink house where there would be a woodstove. We could put on our skates and not freeze our fingers. Sometimes we would get a chance to learn a few new words from the older guys. Later on, I would get to play hockey there and also skate to music. At first, I thought that only sissies skated to music, but then I learned that it was fun and perhaps I was also a sissy. In any case, I found a good dance partner and became a better skater.

It was a lot of fun, and large crowds turned up to take part; however, it was outdoors in Nova Scotia, and the weather played a very big role in activities there. I am not sure how many years the rink remained, but it did create a lot of joy for the people in the community.

There was another very cold winter night when some of us ventured to Middle Musquodoboit for a hockey game. There was always a rivalry between the two communities. Middle was the larger community, so we had to work a little harder to come up with enough good players to compete. They had a nice outdoor rink, and it had more lights on it than the one at home. I don't remember the score of the game so I will assume we lost.

What I do remember very well was the trip back home. As I mentioned, it was very cold. We were all piled in the back of a half-ton truck (the most common method of travel at the time). I would guess there would be five in the cab and many more in the back (which was open). To be fair to the ladies that were with us, we decided the boys should sit on the floor of the truck. Then the ladies could sit on our legs and we would both be more comfortable. Try to picture this. The guys are seated on the floor of the truck. They are situated with their backs to the body of the truck with their feet straight out. Each guy would have at least one, maybe two sitting on his legs. It was extremely cold, and after a short distance, my legs started to get numb from the lack of circulation caused by two ladies who were nesting quite comfortably on them.

I was in a quandary. What should I do? I was enjoying the company of the ladies, yet my feet would surely freeze if I did not free them from that wonderful position. We had another six or seven miles to go, so I decided to let my feet freeze and enjoy the trip as best as I could. After all, how many times does this opportunity present itself to a young lad? I think I must have made the right decision because I never had that experience again, and it has been over fifty-five years since that night. My feet did give me a lot of trouble for a long time after that, but you have heard the expression "No pain, no gain."

Over the years there would be several hockey games around the area. Almost all of these would be spontaneous. Weather became the biggest issue. I really think this added to the excitement of the game, as every event was so uncertain.

One of these games turned out to provide more excitement than we expected. We had been invited to play a game against Elmsvale, a village between Upper Musquodoboit and Middle Musquodoboit. One of the boys from that area boasted they had a team that would whip us real bad. We met on a Saturday morning at 10:00 a.m. They had a good location. It was in an old gravel pit. There were no boards, but the puck could not go far because of the gravel around the sides.

We were a little timid at first, but we knew we had a great goaltender. He did not wear skates, but he could stop just about anything. We played about twenty minutes and scored twelve goals. Our opponents had zero. Someone from their team decided that was enough, and they disappeared. A short time later, the man who owned the gravel pit came and ordered us off his property. He said we were damaging his gravel pit. We left without any incidents, but we were sure the man had been asked out just to save their team from any further embarrassment.

A few years later, a nice rink was provided by Lester Dean in Dean settlement, Nova Scotia, up the road about six miles from Upper Musquodoboit. He had a portion of his pasture dug out in a rectangle about the size of a regular sheet of ice. They had a rink house with a stove as well. They never did get boards around it, but once again, the gravel on the sides helped keep the puck relatively close.

I spent many hours there skating and playing hockey. My wife skated there as did a lot of our friends. I think they had a rule that a good portion of the ice time was to be for skating only. This was a good rule; otherwise, the boys would hog the ice all the time.

One Sunday afternoon, there was a big crowd on hand to skate. A friend of mine, and a well-liked gentleman, came down to skate. I was not sure how good a skater he was, but I was soon to learn. He put his skates on in the rink house, as was the custom, and came out and stood in the door. The rink house was at the end of the ice surface and about four feet up the bank. There was a board ramp from the house to the ice. It had a decline that was rather steep, with small boards nailed across to help the skaters in and out.

When he started down the ramp, someone noticed he had a hockey stick in his hand and called out to him that it was skating time only. Not to worry. It turned out that the stick was purely for balance and not for hockey. He hit the ice running and waving the stick over his head for balance. He went straight across the full length of the ice and right up the gravel bank. He made a clumsy turn and headed for the ice once more. He managed to cross it again without falling and proceeded right up into the rink house, still waving the stick for balance. The rink was crowded, but he never hit a single person.

That was the end of his skating for that year, and perhaps it was his first and last. The large crowd was in stiches, and I am sure the noise could be heard for miles around. I would meet this man many times later on and as he played the fiddle and helped me a great deal with mine. He was an inspiration to me, and I will always remember him.

As I mentioned before, the rink was used for hockey for certain periods of time. There was one occasion when we had a large crowd and had to divide the players into group A and B. This was done in a fair manner, and both sides were happy. I mentioned earlier that there was one fellow who could not skate, but he was a good goaltender. He played most of the time with rubber boots on and wore an old felt hat while he played.

In those days, equipment was very scarce. Uniforms were out of the question, and all protective gear was homemade. Shin pads were almost always magazines. Sometimes it would take two or three for each leg, depending on the availability and sizes of the magazines.

We always had a few rules, but no referees; you followed the rules or else. On this day, we were doing quite well, and nothing beyond a few cuss words were uttered. We had played quite a while when one of the guys forgot one of the rules of the day: Don't lift the puck! He came in on the guy with the rubber boots and felt hat and let a Bobby Hull shot go. It sailed right at the guy with the boots on and about four feet off the ice. The puck hit the old felt hat and took it right off the guy's head. Now you are hearing words that are not fit for tender ears. The goaltender went right to the rink house and stayed there.

It was a sight to behold. Oh, how I wish we could have caught that on video! Everyone was laughing, and Reggie the goaltender was still inside cussing. I get to see Reggie once in a while, and we always get a laugh at this little part of the past.

I skate to where the puck is going to be, not to where it has been.
(Wayne Gretzky)

Skate Sailing on the Meadow

Sometimes if weather conditions were just right, there would be great skating on the old meadow in Upper Musquodoboit. If we got mild weather with a fair amount of rain, the water levels would rise and flood the whole meadow. If the temperature dropped quickly, the water would freeze and create a perfect sheet of ice. If the water receded and the ice was still quite thick, it would still hold up. This was ideal. Over the winter months, this could happen once or twice. The main riverbed would usually be open, so we knew enough to stay away.

I remember one season when all conditions were perfect and we skated all day on the huge meadow. I am only guessing, but I think the area was a half mile wide and almost a mile long. The river ran down closer to one side, so we still had a very large area to skate. On this special day, we tired ourselves out and stopped to rest. While we were doing this, we came up with a new twist. We would each build a sail and let the wind blow us all over the meadow. Now you have to understand something about the geography of our little village. It was about as far away from saltwater as any other place in Nova Scotia. None of us had ever seen a sailboat in our life. We had no idea how they operated. One of the boys had heard about tacking, but did not understand what it meant.

We were determined to give it a try and decided to go home and create something. The plan was to come back the next day and use our sails to propel us along. It was a sight to see when three or four of us showed up the next day. There were all types of contraptions, most of which would scare a normal human being. We did, however, help each other put our sails together. Most of us used cardboard boxes tied onto small boards. The two-by-four had to go. The biggest sail was about four feet by six feet. It was a cool morning with a little snow in the air when we first put on our skates and set out across the meadow. At first, the air was still and the sails were of little use. Soon, however, the good Lord must have wanted to see a funny sight and called for a gust of wind. I was the first one to feel the wind and quickly headed out over the ice. What a thrill to go faster and faster. Each one of us felt the wind on our back as we gained more and more speed. The wind seemed to blow even harder, and soon it became almost scary.

It was a very short time before we had crossed the meadow. The snow had increased by this time and the sky was quite dark. Looking back to the side, we just came from seemed like miles away. Then we realized something. How are we going to get back? Certainly not by the method that got us here. It was at this point that one of the boys shouted. I remember now what that word meant. It was a way of sailing against the wind, but I forget how it was done. It was many years later that we found out what that little word meant and how to perform the task.

We all struggled to get back against the wind and snow. It took us just minutes to get to one side, and it seemed like hours to get back. When we finally reached our original launch site, we were tired little boys. Overall, it was a great adventure, and one we will not forget.

As I finished this little chapter, I realized it was almost 11:00 a.m., November 11, 2013. I can't help but think of all the people who lost their lives while trying to create a safer life for the people back home, just to have a safe country to play in. I also thought how lucky our little group was on the ice that day.

My family, like many others in our little village, lost loved ones, family, and friends during the First and Second World Wars and later, the Korean War. Boys and girls my age were well aware of the war, especially the last few years. We were afraid and uncertain about what would happen. Many soldiers gave their lives so we could live a better life. On this day and every day, we should remember these fallen heroes.

Skating Party

Being a country boy in the late forties and fifties, we did not have the luxury of indoor rinks. We thought we were fortunate to have good ice to skate on when conditions were right. Once in a while we would find a good area, and the party was on.

I remember one Friday evening when we decided to have a skating party. There was never a lot of planning to do; just pick a spot, invite everyone we could, and of course, find an old truck tire or large car tire. The tires were of the utmost importance as they would become our only source of warmth, unless of course we could find a nice young girl to skate with. I always found the tires to be a lot more reliable. On this particular night, we were on a part of the meadow that was close to Mount William. Most of you will not know where this is, and really, it is not that important. I should explain further, however, as it comes to play later. The Mount William I refer to was a large round hill covered with trees, and we were warned to stay away from it at all costs. Legend had it that there was a huge hole at the top of this hill filled with water and that it did not have a bottom. If we ventured too close to it, we could fall in and never be found. It was also reported that there were grave sites there as well. I did venture there once with a few of my friends, but we did not see either sight. I can assure you it was not a place we went to on a regular basis.

Back to the skating party, we had many over the years, but this one seems to stand out in my mind. The ice on the meadow that night was very smooth, but the water had receded about a foot. The ice was sloped from the edge for about a hundred feet. Once we reached the area where the water supported the ice, it was great. The wind was blowing off the land, and it gave us a few problems. One of our skaters who will be referred to as Sid had come along that night although skating was not one of his strong points. He tried to stand up on his dull skates as best as he could and remained close to the fire. Now it is important for everyone to realize that even though there were about a dozen skaters there, most of us did not have new skates nor would we go on to become figure skating champions.

We did know how to keep on our feet most of the time, except for Sid. Some of the boys decided to help him out by skating beside him with one hand under his arm. After a while, he started to master his dull skates and could stand alone. On most nights, the light from the fire would give us light for a radius of thirty or forty feet. Outside of that was total darkness, unless we had a bright moon. After several trial runs for Sid, we invited him to play a fun game, one the rest of us had tried several times. We would skate in a straight line, each skater holding hands with the other with one of the strongest skaters leading the way. We placed Sid at the tail end. The object of the game was to skate as fast as you could, then the leader would dig in his skates and start the rest of the line to swing around. When this was executed properly, each skater in line would go faster and faster. At the end of the line was Sid, who by now was proceeding faster than he had ever before imagined. He lost his grip and flew off into the wild blue yonder with the wind at his back, the rest of us laughing like young fools. We were young fools. We came back and gathered around the fire where we could see again. After several minutes, we realized that Sid was not with us. We yelled, but there was no answer. This went on for another few minutes, and then we started to worry. Someone even suggested that he might have ended up on Mount William and fell in the hole. Then he appeared out of the darkness crawling on his hands and knees. He said that was much easier than trying to skate any further against the wind.

We stayed to watch the last of the tire burn and then set off toward home for a cup of hot cocoa. When we arrived home, we would smell like tire smoke and our eyebrows would be often singed from being too close to the fire. Oh, the fun we had, and we did not hurt a soul.

As I write this, I am wondering how many young people skate on the old meadow now. I think I would like to try it again. At seventy plus, I am years behind already.

A Cave Fit for a King

As young boys, just hanging out together was a lot of fun. There were days we just wandered around the village kicking rocks and old cans. It was a way of being together and wandering the countryside, until we thought of something better to do.

On one of those days, a light went on, and we decided to build ourselves a camp. There was no money or materials. That should have been enough to discourage us, but when you have a group of young boys with nothing to do, sooner or later, one of them will come up with a brilliant idea. We walked on and gave more thought to this soon-to-be successful venture. Then it hit us. By the old river bridge where we played many, many times, there was an old mill site. It had been there for years and was owned by a Mr. Blades. I will sidetrack for a few moments.

I remember the mill very well, as I frequented the site as often as I could, just to hear the old steam mill and smell the new sawn lumber. I always stayed back far enough to keep out of trouble, but close enough to listen and learn. On more than one occasion, one of the workers would take me inside to watch from a better vantage point. It was exciting to watch the logs being cut into lumber. The noise level would never meet today's safety standards, but I did not mind. It was a chance to be part of a big mill operation.

The fireman who worked there was very particular about the steam boiler and kept everything around it very clean and tidy. His name was Jack. I don't think he liked children very much, or perhaps it was a front just to keep us at bay. He always had one or two nice horses that we admired. There is a story I should tell about my father that relates to the old mill.

My father worked on the edger in the mill for a short time. During this time, my stepmother was expecting a new baby any day. The mill was just out the road from our house, and you could look across the field and see it. The mill was enclosed in order to keep out the elements. My father removed one of the wide boards from the side of the mill so he could look over to the house from where he was working. My stepmother had a big red blanket and was to hang this blanket out on the line if she felt she had to go to the hospital. When Dad looked out through the boards on the mill and the red blanket was hanging on the clothesline, it was time to run home. It was a crude way to communicate, but it worked. Can you imagine, they did not have a cell phone!

Now back to the cave. The mill was no longer in use, but there were a few pieces of lumber there and lots of sawdust. Someone had taken the time to level the sawdust pile and push it out toward the river. We decided to forgo the idea of a camp and dig ourselves a cave instead. It was a hard job digging the sawdust out, but in a few days, we had a cave that was about six feet by eight feet and five feet deep. We dug a walkway from our cave toward the riverbank as well. It was about three feet wide. Because of the age of the old sawdust pile, the walls stayed very firm.

While we were digging our cave, we managed to find enough old boards to cover the top and then shoveled sawdust over the boards. We did the same to the entrance. When this was finished, we had a cave that was about five feet high covered with boards and then covered with a foot of sawdust. When complete, we had ourselves a remarkable place to meet in all kinds of weather. If you were seated inside, you could look out through the cave entrance and see the river flowing by.

It was important for all of us to be home on time for meals, so there was no reason to have a lot of food in our abode; but from time to time, a few apples would be found along with biscuits, cookies, etc., just to keep us alive. I don't know how long we used this old cave, and I am not sure how many people even knew it existed. Perhaps Ron, Frank, Alan, Elliot, Keven, and Robert did; but to us, it was our own and we enjoyed our time there.

On more than one occasion, one or two of the young ladies would sneak around to see what we were doing. They would not dare enter the old cave and told us we were crazy. That pleased us to no end because we did not want them there anyway. In later years, we may have tried to entice them in, I suppose; but at this time in our lives, we were much more at ease when they left us alone.

There were many gatherings at the cave, and many tall stories were told. It was an opportunity to share a few jokes and poke fun at one another. In the grand scheme of things, this little cave was very insignificant; but to a small group of boys, it was like a castle. We can't go back to our little cave, but we certainly can remember the fun we had. The boys who were part of this venture have moved to other places, but I am sure they still think about our little hideout.

When life gives you a hundred reasons to cry, show life that you have a thousand reasons to smile. (Unknown)

Dean School Early Fifties

Left to right, Jessie Rogers, Edith Flemming, Vivian Dean, Freda Cox. Front Row. Faye Watson, Jackie Brown.

The Boys in the Trees

This is a story that appeared in my first book, but I thought it deserved another printing. It all took place near Clyde hill, a place close to my heart. We spent countless hours there playing games and exploring. This event came about in the spring of the year. It was a time of the year when the juniper trees were very supple. When the sap started to run, you could bend the little trees right to the ground and they would snap right back when you let them go. To the best of my knowledge, there was never any harm done to the trees. I think these trees actually enjoyed the attention (that is what we wanted to believe).

We would all search for our own tree in that small area and try to climb as far up as we could. The trees we picked for this exercise were about three to five inches in diameter. When we started to climb, the trees would bend more as we got closer to the top. This made the climbing more difficult as the tree would sway back and forth. On a windy day, it was even more of a challenge. The trees would eventually bend right to the ground. When this happened, we would simply let go of the tree and it would stand up straight again, just like nothing ever happened to it. Sometimes we would pair up and find a bigger tree to climb. It was like "double your pleasure."

Around this time of year—I think it would have been the Easter break—we would always be blessed with a visit from a city boy who knew everything there was to know. Not really, he just thought he did. He had an uncle who lived in the area, and his parents sent him to the country for an education. Being good country boys, we did not have much time for this overdressed city boy. Now, it was on one of our tree-climbing capers that he showed up on the scene with his mouth in high gear and, as usual, his brain in neutral. We asked him if he ever climbed one of these juniper trees. He replied that he had climbed much bigger ones in the city and did not think this would be much fun.

We used our best persuasive tactics to get him to climb along with us. It worked and he agreed to give it a try. We found a good tall tree about six inches in diameter. There were three of us aside from the city boy. I believe there was Elliot Whitman, Ronald Decker, and myself. We gave him a few instructions on the ground before we started to climb. The most important was to hang on to the tree as it started to bend toward the ground. Now you have to try to visualize this event. The tree, which is at least twenty-five feet high, is starting to bend toward the earth with four boys hanging on to it. As we were slowly getting closer to the ground, we warned him again, "Don't let go!"

As the first boy touched the ground, the country boys all let go. The tree now whipped back up with the city boy still hanging on. Because of the speed it was traveling, it went past the original upright position and toward the opposite direction. He looked like a flag flying in the wind. After two or three back-and-forth movements, the tree came to rest. He came down that tree like a monkey and told us he thought his uncle needed him at home.

He never bothered us for the rest of his visit. We did not intend to harm him in any way and we didn't. We just wanted to show him that he still had a few things to learn, especially if he wanted to survive in the country. He would show up a few more times in later years, but his attitude had certainly changed. I guess there is a thin line between bullying and our form of teaching. We were not teachers. I think you could call it an exercise in hands on training.

> *Always do right. This will gratify some people and astonish the rest.* (Mark Twain)

School Days

When I look back on the time I spent in school, I am amazed we had so much fun in spite of the fact there were many difficult times. I remember that many of my teachers were very strict and had a zero tolerance for laughter or any other form of disobedience. There would be occasions, however, when a teacher would let their guard down and see the humor in our actions.

I have put together a few examples of these situations and hope that you too will feel the urge to laugh. They are not in any particular order of importance, nor did they take place at the same school. I would like to point out that none of the people included in this book were ever involved in hazing or bullying that I am aware of. We were good friends and never had any intention of harming others. We were pranksters for sure, but we looked out for each other as well. I keep in contact with a few of these boys, and they would all tell you the same. We had fun, we laughed a lot, we teased each other, but we knew the line we had to follow and we did so, assuredly.

The first example to come to mind took place in Hutchinson School. I was in grade five. I remember it well. It was in the afternoon. I know this because we went to school from 1:00 to 5:00 p.m. that year. The school was overcrowded, and the total enrolment was cut in half—one group in the morning, the other in the afternoon.

This story will be called "A Pop for the Class." I had several cousins attending this school, and one of them was Curry. Curry could make this strange popping sound by placing his finger inside his mouth and then turning the finger sideways, snapping it out along the side of his cheek. When he did so, it would make a resounding *pop*. We knew he practiced this over and over as he was good at it. Now this was not the first time anyone had done this. I am sure children all over the world had taken a turn at it, but let me tell you, Curry was good.

One day, he decided he had perfected it to a point that he could try it in class. The sound was tremendous. We were all trying to keep our cool as we saw the teacher's eyes go around the room, searching for the culprit. Finally, she saw what must have been the look of success, as well as fear, in Curry's eyes. She was very cool about it all and pleasantly spoke. "Curry, would you please come up to my desk." When he approached her desk, she spoke again. "Curry has learned something new, and I am sure he would like to demonstrate for you. Curry, please show the class what you can do." He tried and he tried, but not a sound could we hear. After a long pause, we could see a tear running down his cheek. The teacher must have seen this as well and advised him to go back to his seat and in the future refrain from such antics.

He was not in his seat one minute when we heard the sweetest pop of all. We looked around to see Curry with the biggest smile one could imagine. The teacher did not say a word. I think she must have felt he had learned a lesson and did not need to be punished any further. I am sure Curry was pleased with his effort after he returned to the confines of his own seat and would move on to other adventures in the future.

A short time after this, another cousin of mine, Lorne, teamed up with me to fetch a pail of water for the school. This might seem like a simple task, but not so. The school did not have hot and cold running water. In fact, there was no water at all. The boys were always selected in tandem to go to the farmhouse behind the school for the water. This was not an easy task as it was a long walk through the pasture. The pasture was covered with bushes and small trees. There were hills and valleys along the way, not to mention the piles of manure. There was one ditch that had caused problems for a few of the boys so a bridge was built to make travel a little easier. This bridge was just an old door that had served its time and now was a makeshift bridge. It was fun to go for the water as the people on the farm were nice to us, and it was a chance to get out of school for at least a few minutes. I think the round trip was about fifteen minutes if we did not go too fast.

On this occasion, we made sure we enjoyed nature at its best. Lorne and I took turns carrying the bucket full of water back to the school; this was the reason for two boys going in the first place. We had picked up the fresh water at the farm and were on our way back. Lorne said to me, "Did you ever swing a full bucket of water over your head without spilling any water?" I had heard about it, but I had never tried it. I was not about to do it on this day as it was cold and snowing a little at the time. As we approached the little bridge, he said, "I am going to do it right here on the bridge." He started to swing the bucket back and forth, back and forth, each time trying to get the swinging motion going. By this time, it had snowed enough that the surface of the bridge was covered. As he was in one of his forward motions, he lost his footing on the slippery bridge and went down on his rear end. The bucket was empty in an instant, and his pants had soaked up a fair share of the water. We were faced with the task of going back to the farm for another bucket of water. We would have to move much faster now as we had used up our allotted time and as yet we did not have the water.

When we finally reached the school, the teacher was upset with us, but when she heard we had a delay because of the slippery bridge, she decided not to punish us. We neglected to tell her about the little experiment that caused our delay.

On another day during recess, one of the boys said he would like to put his foot through the window. We were in the boys' cloakroom and the window was just about waist high. The window consisted of one large window with several smaller panes of glass. Geordie lifted his leg and placed his foot right up against the glass. I just happened to be behind him and gave him a gentle nudge. With this, he lost his balance and actually put his foot right through the pane of glass, just like he said he wanted to do. The noise alerted the teacher, and she came running to see what happened. Geordie told her that I broke the window. His leg was still out through the broken window. After a short time of listening to him try to convince her it was not his fault, I confessed it was just as much my fault as his.

We were both chastised and ordered to have the window fixed the next day before school. We somehow got enough money together to buy the glass and fix the broken window on time. I think the glass cost us fifteen cents. That, my friends, was a lot of money for two small schoolboys in1950.

The next year, we had a new teacher. She had an alarm clock on her desk with the front of the clock facing her. We could not see the time, so we could only guess how much longer before we could leave school and get on with much more important matters. In those years, it was very unusual for students to have a watch.

One day before school (we were still in the afternoon class until five in the afternoon), we came upon the idea of speeding up our day by adjusting the clock just a little. Now I know this is not new. We were not on the cutting edge of technology, but it seemed like a good idea at the time. The pencil sharpener was on her desk quite close to the clock, so we had an excuse to go up to her desk at least once a day to sharpen our pencils. One of the boys determined which way to turn the hands by turning the mechanism on the back. It was a simple plan: just go up to her desk and sharpen your pencil and give the clock a little boost. Not too much at one time, or the teacher would be sure to notice. When we decided to set this plan in motion, the girls were left out. We felt they would surely tell the teacher and all would be lost. We started our afternoon off with high expectations as we were quite sure we would get out early and be gone. This was not meant to be. The day seemed to be longer than usual. As we waited for the bell to ring, we noticed that it seemed to be getting dark quite early. When the bell finally rang, we ran out and headed home. When I arrived home, it was five thirty. We were all in school at least another fifteen minutes. When we were turning the hands on the clock, most of us were turning them the wrong way. Our teacher must have known, but she never said a word. She did move her clock to the other side of the desk, but we could not reach it. It was clearly an occasion where the teacher got the best of the boys.

The Essay

This story is about one of our good friends who could always find a quiet way to get us into fits of laughter. We were in our English class and giving our teacher our undivided attention. She informed us that we were to have an essay ready for Monday morning. It was to be about something we did on the weekend. Now this was on Friday so we did not have a lot of preparation time. This was not the sort of thing we wanted over our heads all weekend. We all felt we were being robbed of our valuable personal time. Well, we were in a situation we did not like, but we decided to do our best. Sid, however, was not your average guy. He decided he would consider the odds before he started his essay. On the long bus ride home from school, he discussed his plan with a few of his close friends. There was Warren, Aubrey, and one or two more who heard his plan. He felt that the odds of him having to read his essay were very small. You see, there were about twenty people in the class, and the teacher would never get around to asking all of us to read. He also was quite sure that the teacher would not read them all even if she did ask to have them turned in. His final decision after careful thought was to take his chance and not do a thing.

When Monday arrived, we went right to English class. The teacher shot Sid's theory down in a few seconds. "Now, class, we are going to hear you read your weekend assignments. Sidney, how would you like to be first?" I was seated beside Sid, and all I could do was try not to laugh too loud. He opened his notebook very slowly and stood there for what seemed like a long time. I could see there was not a word on the paper. Finally, he spoke. (He was always a slow talker so we did not expect a great deal of speed.) "Today, I want to tell you about my dog Sport . . ." Long pause. "My dog is a good dog." Long pause again. "My dog follows me around the farm. He likes it on the farm where he can run and play.

He helps bring in the cattle at night." Now he is on a roll and actually increases the tempo. He went on a little longer until the teacher spoke. She must have sensed the he was up to no good but did not pursue it any further. I am sure she had a hard time keeping her cool knowing that he was probably faking it. She told all of us to pass in our assignment, and that was the end of it.

We all had a great laugh later on. We all learned from Sid the real meaning of flying by the seat of your pants or winging it. I think if Sid had to do it over, he would have completed his homework. Our teacher was a great teacher, and I never forgot the gentle way she handled things that day. I bet she had fun telling her fellow teachers all about this when she got back to the teachers' room that day.

Garfield and the Chair

We are back to high school now and another story about a teacher's forgiveness. We were in a class with Mr. Best He was a good teacher, but prone to a few antics of his own. One of the boys in the class, Garfield, was seated at the back of the class. He was trying to take in all the information he could that day (if you believe that I have a great land deal for you). Garfield had pushed his chair back just a little and tipped it back. For some unknown reason, the chair slipped out from under him and he crashed to the floor. Mr. Best did not even check to see if he was hurt, but shouted, "Out, out, young man! Get out of my class this instant!" Garfield left the class.

Two weeks later, we were all back in Mr. Best's class. He was wandering around the class talking about our lessons for the next week. He went up to his desk, put one foot on his chair, and attempted to lean back. In doing so, he crashed to the floor in a heap. In an instant, Garfield jumped to his feet and spoke harshly, "Get out, get out of this class!" We were all laughing, but cautiously waited for a severe reprimand. When Mr. Best got up off the floor and adjusted his glasses, he said with a grin, "Now, class, where were we?" If I had been that teacher, I would have been too embarrassed to speak. The whole thing was funny, and no one was hurt. I had great respect for the way the teacher handled us and got us back on track. Garfield got even with the teacher and without any repercussions.

It may seem like our only interest in school was to raise havoc, but that was not the case. I could tell you at great length all about our French lessons, English lessons, mathematics, etc., but you would soon put the book away. I always found that relaxing and having a little fun made me want to learn more. My best days in school were the days when we had fun. It was on one of those days that one of the boys came to school with a few hairpins. Some referred to them as bobby pins. It would soon turn into a musical afternoon. We broke the pins into two parts. Each part would produce a sound of its own. Our school desks had a slot just under the top where the legs met. One could insert the pins there without being readily seen. When the pins were inserted, we could change the pitch of sound by shoving the pins farther into the slot. If each one of the many boys adjusted them properly, there would be a unique sound for each boy.

The plan was very simple. We set up these instruments of sound before the class began. We were situated in various seats throughout the class. We had a system worked out to cause the teacher to travel from one side of the room to the other. A boy in the back would strike a chord, then one in the front would follow. And on and on. Our teacher that day was a very nice gentleman, but I think we may have gone a little too far. When he heard the first note, he stopped and listened. He knew what it was right away. He did not know where it originated, but he knew what it was. He casually walked around the room while talking about our French lesson. When he got to the back of the class, the notes rang out at the front. When he moved toward the front, the sound came from the back. We knew it could not go on forever, but we were doing quite well. He started to pace around the room faster and faster, watching our every move. Finally, he stopped and shouted, "That is enough! If this noise does not stop now, everyone in this room will go to detention." We had our fun, but none of us wanted detention, and we did not want to harm our teacher. To the best of my knowledge, we gave him our undivided attention for the rest of that year. Fun, learning, and laughter do go well together.

During this same time, we had several other tricks we would play on each other. Our good friend Gordon was one to get out of each class as fast as he could. We never found out why he was in such a hurry, but he was always ready to go as soon as the buzzer sounded. He did not carry the traditional book bag, but tied his books together with a leather belt. The belt would be around the bottom and fastened at the top, with about six inches left over for a convenient handle. He always put his loose-leaf binder on the bottom. Then he would put a few scribblers on top of the binder. His books were next, and there was usually four. This made a very neat bundle. He was meticulous in his effort to have everything in place before he left each class. He always tried to sit in the seat nearest to the door. His books were always at the front of his desk so he could grab the end of the belt and be off out the door as soon as the class ended.

On more than one occasion, the evils of sabotage would move in. When Gordon reached his class, he would loosen the belt and take out whatever was needed for this particular class. Just before the end of the class, he would replace all the material, fasten the belt tight, and be off.

During the break between classes, at least one or two of us would move close to Gordon's desk. One would somehow catch his attention while another would rig his books. It was easy. All that had to be done was simple. The ring binder was always on the bottom. Take the belt he used to tie it all together, put it under the top of the binder, and leave the rest of the belt loose on top of the pile just as he left it. As soon as the class was over, he would tighten the belt and be gone out the door and down the corridor. It was always a pretty sight. He would run out the door with papers flying out of the binder. By the time he discovered the problem and gathered up all the loose pages, he was at the back of the line and not in his desired place at the front. We played this trick on him several times, but each time we had more difficulty as he watched us like a hawk. You could fool him once, but after that, he kept his eye on you forever after. It was not always the boys who did this. The girls seemed to have more success. I guess he did not think they would stoop so low.

Gordon was good at being on the receiving end and equally good at handing it out. We were all close friends and enjoyed the little pranks. It was all part of the growing process, and hopefully, no serious harm was done.

There were other occasions when we became victims of circumstances. In our high school days, punishment was sometimes extreme. Let me give you a few examples. During a break between periods, I was approaching the water fountain for a drink. One of my friends gave me a push. I lost my balance, stepped out of line, and was easily seen by the principal. He called me over and ordered me to walk from one end of the school to the other and back, stepping on the center line of tile. The main corridor was about seventy-five feet long. There were two wings that were about fifty feet. The tiles on the floor were nine-inch tiles. I had to walk both ways with students watching and never missed a single tile.

The principal made an example of me. That is the way it was. I had no recourse. We had to walk in single file at all times. Break that rule for any reason and you were punished. At the time, I was very hurt and embarrassed over this incident, but now I sometimes wish our teachers had that much power again.

There was another time the boys were all ordered into the gymnasium. It had been discovered that someone had made a mess on one of the toilets in the boys' washrooms. The principal asked the person or persons who were responsible to step forward. No one obliged. After one more request and still silence from the large group, he informed us he had a plan. He had a number in his head. He made us all line up along the wall of the gym. He ordered us to start counting from the left. The count began. When the count got to me, he stopped counting to announce I was the one who would have to clean the toilets. The number was 57. I will never forget that number as long as I live. I cleaned every toilet, and from that day on, I waited for someone to let out a clue as to who the guilty person was. That never happened. Why would the guilty one come forward? They knew the odds were certainly in their favor to escape punishment if they kept their lips sealed.

On several occasions, the gym floor would get marked due to people being on it with street shoes (usually black marks). On most of these occasions, the principal would again order the boys into the gym and select three or four to clean all the marks. We were given a rag and a small container of gasoline. Down on our hands and knees we went and cleaned the spots. What would happen to a school principal today if those techniques were used? I am glad this type of discipline has been erased, but perhaps we have let the pendulum swing too far. Later on in my high school years, I would develop a solid respect for this principal in spite of the pain he had inflicted on me.

In my last year of school, I was summoned to his office. I was scared for sure. In my previous years and all my antics, I had never been in his office. He was brief and to the point. "Robert, it is now March and your marks are very low. You do not have a hope of passing." My thoughts went from fear to anger, and I decided to tell him how upset I was. He listened to me for a few moments, and I saw the very slightest hint of a smile. I was smart enough to realize he was challenging me. He knew I had the ability, but I was not moving in the right direction. I told him that I would pass and that I would not be near the bottom of my class. He knew what he was doing, and he gave me the push I so badly needed. I finished the year with good marks and a smile on my face.

It is important to put a lot of years into your life, but also important to put a lot of life into your years.

99

Richard Price, Robert Taylor, and Gordon Danes. On
the way to Melmerby Beach. May 24th 1956.

Richard was best man at our wedding. I was also his best man at his
wedding a little later on. Gordon was one of our good friends. Both of
these gentlemen died early in life.

Hutchinson School 1943

Back row. Alice Hutchinson, Norma Stewart, Teacher Marion Farnell, Donnie Fraser, Betty Fraser, Joyce Fraser, Edith Hutchinson, and Joan Logan.

Second row. Dorothy Erskine, Beverly Whitman, Joan Gilbert, Barbara Holman, Kaye Flemming, Marie Fraser, Ester Flemming, Roberta Grant, Shirley Erskine, Joan Stewart.

Front row. Royce Higgins, Cam Brown, Hugh Erskine, Donald Erskine, Geordie Grant Willard Erskine, Ronnie Higgins, Gerald Gilbert, and Perry Logan.

The goal is not to live forever, but to create things that will.
(Unknown)

The Kick under the Table

This is a story that has at least one lesson to be learned. Not all the things we did in school were part of the learning curve, unless you want to include the expenditure of excess energy by a bunch of growing boys. This story took place in the high school library. Now I am sure most teachers would agree that a library is not really a place for young boys to be contained for any great length of time. Being quiet and seated at a table where silence is the rule is a great way to guarantee some sort of trouble.

On this particular day, we had just finished a class in the gymnasium and rushed to our library class. Several boys were seated at a table on the opposite side of the room and quite a few feet from the teacher on duty. Most of us had plans to prepare for our next class; however, one boy had other ideas. He decided to kick one of the other boys on the shin. It was easy to do this as the huge tables gave lots of room to swing your feet, and it was easy to hit your intended target. Gordon was the one who started the events that led to a visit to the principal. He kicked the boy directly across from him and hit his target dead-on. There was a muffled sound from the target, but not loud enough to catch the teacher's attention. After a few moments, Gordon launched his next kick, and this one was much harder. The muffled sound became a curse, and this time the teacher saw fit to do some investigating.

She walked quietly to our desk and told us we should remember where we were and should study in silence. After she had returned to her desk, it was quiet again, but you must realize one of us had been kicked twice and the second kick was hard enough to hurt just a little. Our friend Sid was the one who received the first punishing blow, so he decided it was time to return the favor. Now Sid was strong, and he prepared for a tremendous fling of his big foot. This time, the silence was broken with a yell so loud everyone in the library heard it. The teacher raced down again and demanded to know who had yelled. Gordon reluctantly told her it was his fault. She said, "Gordon, one more outburst like this and you are off to the principal's office."

"Yes, Teacher," he replied. We were having a hard time controlling ourselves and knew that this was not the end of the kicking under the table. Remember, the score is two kicks to one. After a few more minutes, Sid must have decided it was time to even the score. He let go with a kick that landed just below Gordon's knee. This time, the yell was more loud. "Jesus!" Gordon exclaimed. This time, the teacher walked slowly to Gordon and told him to stand outside the library door and wait for further punishment after the class. The rest of us were in stiches but maintained our composure, as we really had nothing to do with the whole thing but enjoyed it immensely.

Gordon was given a reprimand after class, but nothing worse. The lesson to be learned is quite simple. If you wear soft-soled shoes, don't be kicking anyone who is wearing big leather street shoes. Sid always wore hard shoes unless he was in the gym. Gordon just failed to provide the heavy artillery. He started the attack but lost in the end.

There would be other days and other adventures. We were just young boys who had energy to expel and did so without malice. I have very fond memories of the days we were together and miss the boys who are no longer with us.

Water Everywhere

To say I was not a good student would be far from the truth. I was always obedient and had great respect for my teachers. I was always willing to learn as much as I could. Sometimes when the subject was of a nature I disliked or felt little need to know, I would be less than attentive. It was probably on one of those days when our thoughts turned to other things and little time was left for learning.

We were changing classes and were headed for a lesson in the science room. We had five minutes between each class, so we did have a short period of time to act up if the teacher was not in his or her room. On this day, the teacher was not in the class when we arrived. At the back of this class, there was a small room where a variety of plants were growing. Some of us decided to go in and investigate. The group was mostly boys, but one or two girls came in as well. Charley spotted a garden hose with a small nozzle on it and decided to have some fun. He placed the end of the hose between his legs and called to one of the girls to get their attention. Everyone in the room watched him. Most were laughing but a few were shocked. (That's what they said at the time.)

Not being one to miss a chance to increase the level of entertainment, I slipped in behind Charley and found the shutoff valve. It was closed, of course, so I opened it for just a few seconds. The room broke into a loud laughter as Charley tried to hold the water back. He cupped his hand over the nozzle, but the water just spewed out sideways. His pants were wet, and there was water everywhere. We all turned to the next task in an instant and cleaned the water and left the room in fine condition. We made it back to our seats and were none the worse for our excitement. Charley was wet and still in a stupor over the water tap and who turned it on, but I think he had an idea it was soon to be determined.

Did I learn a lot in class that day? Perhaps not. We did learn about teamwork, however, as everyone in class ran to the room to help. On that day, the class bonded even more, and I am sure most of the people there that day will always remember that special day in science class.

Shop Class with Mr. Blackburn

For me to have a good day at school was a real treat. This was one of those days. We were off to Mr. Blackburn's shop class. First, I should tell you a little about our teacher. He was always very informative and willing to teach those of us who were interested. He would often stray from the subject of woodworking, plumbing, heating, etc., just to talk about hockey or some other sport. As boys, we loved the little diversion from the regular studies. He was always one of my favorites, but I think the biggest reason for this was my love for an opportunity to work with my hands. I could hardly wait for his class, and I hung on to every word of instruction he had to offer. Actually, attending his class was like spending time with my dad.

My father was a very gifted individual and had the ability to make anything he wanted without a lot of tools or supplies. In later years, I would hear from a gentleman who knew him well. He said, "Your father was a man who could do anything he set his mind to and did it well." It was a very kind comment from a man who obviously knew him.

It was always so interesting to just follow him around and learn so many skills. When I was ten years old, he decided to build a new house. It was to be a new house out of old lumber. He worked every day after a hard day's work at the old saw mill by the Cariboo Road. (He would later start his own company as a true jack-of-all-trades.) I would help as much as a ten-year-old could, but more important, I learned from the smartest man I ever knew. There were no power tools. Just a hammer and a handsaw. The house is still there and is owned by my brother Dennis.

I mention this now as it was the early part of my interest in working with my hands. Now, back to shop class with Mr. Blackburn. Each year, he would have a spring cleanup, and all the boys who were scheduled for a class on that day took part. Nothing was left untouched, and he was very determined to make sure his shop was in top shape when we were finished. I can only remember one of these adventures because there would be one major cleanup per year and several classes to choose from.

On this one occasion, we were to work in pairs. I was given the opportunity to work with Charley Bates. That was a circus. We were to clean all the light fixtures in the shop. The lights hung from the ceiling, which was about twelve feet high. They were attached to the ceiling with huge chains, one on each end of a four-foot light. There was a large shade over each light. Our job was simple: get a stepladder and a large brush. One of us was to hold the ladder, and the other was to go up and clean the light. This worked quite well for a few lights with me holding the ladder and Charley doing the cleaning. Then Charley decided to drop the brush on my head as I was having a look around the shop. This was a great treat for him to see me in a bit of distress and uttering some unkind words that were certainly meant for him. I waited for him to go back up the ladder, and as he got up to the next light, I shook the ladder just enough to scare him. He quickly grabbed one of the chains on the light and crawled right up on top of the light like a monkey. When he did this, I moved the ladder to the next light and left him high and dry. We were both laughing as he tried to quietly coax me back. The conversation went something like this: "Robert, get back here and let me down." "Charley, stay up there until you wise up." "Get me down out of here before Mr. Blackburn catches us." "Okay, Stubb (this was his nickname). I am going to get you down, but no more fooling around."

We finished that chore without anyone else seeing us and lived to tell the tale many times. I am sad to say Charles passed away a few years back. He was a great guy and always good for a laugh. We were just growing boys at the time, and laughing seemed to make the same process much more fun.

I still have a small metal box I made in my first year in shop class. Mr. Blackburn told me it was the best one of the group. During a class reunion a few years ago, I visited his shop for one last visit before the school was demolished. It was one of the major highlights of the reunion for me.

Before the high school was built, Mr. Blackburn drove a shop mobile. He would visit several of the rural schools in the area with his big green-and-yellow machine. It resembled a huge bus, but it was filled with a variety of woodworking tools. I was not old enough to attend the classes on shop day, as it was for grades seven and above (I think he came every two weeks). I yearned for the chance to take part and loved to see it arrive. There is one just like it in a museum in Pictou County, Nova Scotia. I had an opportunity to visit the museum, and like a child, I bounced into the old shop mobile and my thoughts flew back to a ten-year-old boy. I did not want to leave. You will find a photo of a shop mobile at the end of this chapter, courtesy of the Nova Scotia Museum of Industry, Stellarton, Nova Scotia.

There were many good days in that class, and Mr. Blackburn helped us all. Safety was always foremost in his shop, and he watched over us with pride. There were one or two boys in our class who were not handy with equipment and found themselves working on very simple tasks. Charley was one of those boys. He was smart and had lots of energy, but he liked to channel his energy toward more exciting events. He decided he would build a checkerboard. He used a very simple method, and I am sure the teacher was pleased that he leaned in this direction.

His board consisted of one piece of black Masonite, sixteen inches by sixteen inches. His plan was to line the board off in equal squares and then paint every second one red. Mr. Blackburn helped him set up an easel to make it easier to paint the squares. The first time he tried to paint, he found it very hard to follow the lines and was wiping paint off on a regular basis. After a long time, he started to get the hang of it and things were going smoothly, until the rest of us decided to have some fun with him.

We would wait until he was concentrating on his work and then decide which one of us would sneak up on him and give his arm a little nudge. We had to be very careful not to be seen by Charley or the teacher. The first time was a complete success, and Charley uttered a few very unkind words to his attacker. He would then go to the paint room, try to wipe the damaged area, and come back to his bench. There was always an unwritten code between school boys, especially "don't tell the teacher." Charley adhered to this code. This ritual continued for many weeks after, but I do believe he finished his project before the school year was over.

Charley was well liked by everyone in our class and was often involved in our antics. In all the years I knew him, he was never malicious in any way.

I lost contact with him for several years, and then by sheer coincidence, I heard his name mentioned. A friend of mine from my work mentioned a Charley Bates from Middle Musquodoboit. I told my friend I knew him well and asked him to say hello to Charley for me. They had met at the racetrack. The following week, Vernon told me Charley said he did not know a Bob Taylor from high school. I told Vernon to call Charley a "Stubb" the next time he saw him and watch his reaction. Vernon did this, and Charley laughed and said he must know me for sure. After some more thought, he exclaimed, "Oh, you mean Robert Taylor! No one ever called him Bob in school." Later, I met Charley at the exhibition in Middle Musquodoboit, and we had a great talk. I am very glad we got together. He was a great friend, and I miss him. Nicknames were very common in those days, and in some cases, we would forget their real names. I still see a few of these friends and greet them with a nickname.

This next story has nothing to do with Mr. Blackburn or his shop class, but it did have a huge impact on my younger years. We are sent to school to learn, and for the most part, we do just that. It is not always easy, and sometimes we falter a little in the process. I have mentioned the principal telling me I would not pass my last year of school. When he told me this, something told me he was wrong and I would show him. We were both winners because he motivated me and I responded by bringing my marks up to an acceptable level.

There was one occasion when I was criticized for something and I went the other way. There comes a time in almost every boy's life when "boy meets girl." For a lot of years, I got along just fine, and then a young girl comes into view and all things change. Her name is not important as what I am telling is not new. Every boy or girl who went to high school goes through the same thing. In my case, I expected great things to come my way. That did not happen, and in the process I started to doubt my personal ability. I loved sports in high school. I was not the best, but I loved to play. Then I developed a feeling of insecurity.

During one of our gym classes, we were introduced to dancing. I wanted to learn, and I was very pleased to find out that my new girlfriend was to be my partner. I will never forget the words she used as we were dancing to the "Tennessee Waltz." She said, "You are so stupid you will never learn to dance." For a long time, I thought she was right. I lost a lot of valuable time because I had actually listened to her. I was a little country boy. What did I know?

Well, I am still a little country boy, but I am proud to be just that. I did learn to dance many years later. I also play the fiddle, and I can play the "Tennessee Waltz." This story has a funny tie to the closing of our old high school.

A great old time band I play with was invited to play for a closing dance at the school. It was especially fun to go there as we would see so many of our old classmates. We played in the gymnasium, and there was a very large crowd on hand. I saw the lady who called me stupid and decided to play the waltz. I had told the others in the band about this, and one of them said, "I hope you are not going down there to dance with that lady (those were not the exact words used)."

I did not go down to dance. I had gone beyond those times, and I had grown a lot. To this day, I do not use that hurtful word. I am still that young boy at heart, but I think I am a lot wiser. There are some, I am sure, who will doubt that. Overall, my high school days were a lot of fun. We were young and at times a little group of devils, but I think we recognized right from wrong. We also had the utmost respect for our teachers. I may be old-fashioned, but I think our society has lost some of that respect that is so vitally important.

This photo has been provided by the Nova Scotia Museum of Industry, Stellarton, Nova Scotia. It is on display there and is a wonderful vehicle. See back cover for full color.

The Hunting Trails

For the most part, this book has been about stories including people around me. This, however, is about some of my time alone. I did get to spend a lot of time alone while I was growing up. Some of that time I was lonesome, but a lot of the time, I appreciated the chance to be on my own. When I was walking along the familiar trails in the woods, it was my time to think about and reflect on events in my life. It was a good chance to consider my future or just enjoy the moment.

I was never an avid hunter, but there was a time in my life that I spent many hours in the woods and along the river. It became a way of life for me in my early teenage years. When the hunting season opened in the fall, I came home from school, changed my clothes, put a couple of apples in my pocket, and off I went. I had a certain area that I traveled in every day if it was fit to do so.

I enjoyed hunting for partridge along the old trails and roads. For me, it was a time to relax and enjoy the natural countryside. If I shot a partridge or two, that was a bonus. Most times out, I would get one or two, but I don't remember feeling bad If I did not see any. I would stay out until it started to get dark and then I would be on my way back home. When the deer season was over (I never hunted deer), it was time for rabbits. I hunted rabbits and snared them as well. I followed a trail that I considered my own. I always carried a twelve-gauge shotgun and lots of wire for snares. In order to walk to the area where my snares were set, check them all, and return home, I would have walked about two miles.

I made many trips along this trail, a trail that took me past Clyde hill, the trees we used to swing in, the brook where my brother Mac and I played many times, and through the old property on Fraser hill where I had once lived. On one special day, as I was walking along the trail to look at my snares, something happened that I will never forget. As I approached the narrow path where my first snare was set, I saw the biggest owl I had ever seen. He was frantically beating his wings trying to get off the ground. As I looked closer, I noticed he had not only my rabbit but also the snare and pole along with it. By this time, he had managed to get airborne with his cargo. While this was all taking place, I managed to get a shell into my old shotgun. My intention was to shoot the owl and of course retrieve my rabbit. This was not meant to be. In my haste to get a shot away, I must have aimed a little low as I missed the owl and shot the rabbit into a million pieces. When this happened, the owl's weight decreased an amount equal to the weight of the rabbit. With this decrease in weight, the owl lifted like a helicopter. I think he would have a claw or two missing and would need a hearing aid for the rest of his life.

I was mad because I lost the rabbit, but it was worth the loss just to see that owl take off. To those of you who are avid hunters, you might be wondering how I could blast the rabbit so bad with one shot. The answer is quite simple! SSG. If you still don't understand, you are a lot younger than I.

It was during one of my partridge-hunting trips that I ventured into an area I was not familiar with and got lost. I was hunting along a country road that I had been on several times before, but it was farther along than I was used to. I heard a vehicle coming, and I stepped off into the woods. I did not want to be seen. I walked far enough in to be out of sight from the road. It was cloudy that afternoon, and darkness was closing in.

This departure from the road was caused by the SSGs. Dad had given me these old shotgun shells to use for target practice as they had been declared illegal. I was afraid to be caught with them, so I hid when I heard a vehicle approaching. Now back to my dilemma. In a few minutes, I was lost. I decided to sit and think it out. I knew I was close to the road, but I had no idea which way it was. It is strange how one can learn so many things from one little error. I looked for a tree to climb in the hope of seeing through to the road. I found a suitable tree and had just started to climb when I heard another vehicle. I came down fast, grabbed my gun, and headed for the sound. This time, I was in sight of the road when a car passed; I was quite sure I had not been seen. By this time, I was late and I did not want my stepmother to worry so I ran home. Every time I went on those trips, I was always sure to come home at the same time so she would not worry. I guess that is why I am always punctual to this day. I traveled this trail many times, and each time, I saw a different picture and felt a different feeling. Every step helped to create something new: a change in the wind, a few drops of rain, the sun shining through the tree branches, and on a few occasions new falling snow. All of these changed the landscape and made the travel so much more enjoyable. I felt like it was my own special trail. It was during these walks through the woods that I started to appreciate just how beautiful the country is.

There would be many trips along my trail before I left my home in Upper Musquodoboit. It was my own little world. It was good physical exercise and soul cleansing as well. I loved those days. I know that to go back there would be sad for me as things have changed so much; however, I can still close my eyes and see it all.

I still walk as often as I can and enjoy the solitude. It is a time to think and a time to dream. Our dreams may not all come to fruition, but we should never stop dreaming.

Around this same time in my life, I learned how to trap muskrats. My father had a few old traps, and I was fascinated with them. I asked him if I could have them, and he agreed. He also took me to the river and showed me how to set the traps. We had a short part of the river as lots of people there were trapping close by. I got permission from the farmer who owned the field along the river to trap on his property. The first season I got four muskrats. I was so excited. I would be rich. At that time, there was a gentleman who came around buying pelts. He named a price and that was it. You could haggle perhaps, but his offer gave me the feeling I would never have to get a job the rest of my life. I got $7.50 for them. To add to my riches, I got .25¢ for each pair of rabbits I sold. I think my total combined was $7.75, I will let you do the math. The following year, I did not get a thing so I decided to give up the fur trade for good.

No one can go back and start a new ending, but anyone can start now and make a new ending.

Grandfather Taylor Wittenburg Nova Scotia.

The Working Years

For most of my working years, I was employed by the Canada Post Corporation. They were not all good years; however, I had ample opportunity to learn and advance. I retired after thirty-three years, and I must say the overall experience was a good one. The people we work with determine how well we like our workplace. Over the years, I met more than a few lazy, shiftless characters; however, they were the small minority. I was fortunate enough to meet large numbers of hardworking individuals who were very devoted to the corporation.

One of the people I met and worked with for several years was Vernon Blois. He became a great friend and a mentor to me. Vernon had spent several years as a railway mail clerk. (These people were looked upon as the elite workers in our system. They sorted mail on the trains as they rolled along the tracks.) It was the position most people sought because of the respect that came with the job. In those days, every employee was tested at least once a year. The railway mail clerks had to achieve the highest marks.

This service was discontinued many years ago, and for this reason, many of this elite group came back into a post office to finish their career. It was during this time I met several of them, but Vernon was the one who became an instant hit. He was a very dedicated worker that you could put your entire trust in. He was also a clown. This man had more ways to make one laugh than anyone I ever met. There are so many stories to tell.

Vernon would never lift a finger to harm anyone, but he would go out of his way to lift one's spirits. He would put a plan together at least once a week to cause us to burst out in laughter. As we were on shift work at the time, most of the fun began during the late hours. It was always an exciting time when we stopped for lunch as we never knew what was coming next. I should point out that most of his little surprises worked best when we had at least one or two gullible people to take part. On this occasion, he came to work all prepared. He had found a set of false teeth at home. I think they were an old pair that belonged to his departed mother. He took a pair of pliers and broke several of the teeth off. To this, he added several packages of catsup. (They were still in the packs.) When he arrived at work, he found an accomplice and gave him the complete plan. The whole event would take place while we were all gathered for lunch. There was a normal complement of six or seven people at work at this time. When we broke for lunch, most of us would go downstairs to our lockers pick up our lunch, coffee, tea, etc., and return upstairs to eat.

Vernon and his accomplice, Jack, were the last two people to come upstairs. There was a door at the top of the stairway that opened out right where we were seated. Jack came through the door first and slammed the door in Vernon's face, or so we thought (it was a setup). Vernon came through the doorway with his head down and moaning very loudly. He stood there in front of us and let one or two teeth fall from his mouth. He also let a little catsup run down over his chin. I was not too sure he was hurt but wanted to see what was going to take place. One of the other fellows was very concerned. He cried out, "Hey, you guys, this man is hurt. I'm telling you he is hurt. Don't be laughing at the poor man." About that time, we could see a smile on Vernon's face, and we knew it was a hoax. Once the fellow that was so concerned found out what had happened, he laughed until tears ran down his cheeks. That was one of many events that made our working hours a lot more pleasant.

Late one evening (we were on the midnight shift), he came in with another bag that contained an old phone with the spiral cord still attached. He did not let us know what he had in the bag until the gag was upon us. Vernon was an avid Montreal Canadiens fan, and on this occasion, the Canadiens were in the play-offs with Chicago. He was scheduled to work at midnight so he had to leave home before the game was over. At that time, the evening shift was still working, so there was an overlap of employees for an hour and one half. This gave Vernon a larger audience for his show. I was the supervisor of the midnight shift, and Clayton was supervisor of the evening shift. It was customary for the midnight shift to come in a little early. That way, they could assess the workload for the rest of the shift and, of course, exchange friendly conversation with their fellow workers.

It was during this time that Vernon and his one accomplice started their plan. We were all gathered around the supervisor's desk and not paying much attention to Vernon. Without any of us noticing, he placed his old phone, which was identical to the regular phone, on the desk cradle. He put the office phone in the desk drawer, being very careful to hide the cord. He was very careful to place the old phone cord under the desk cradle. With a little nod to his accomplice, which none of us noticed, the accomplice went downstairs and dialed the phone number at the supervisor's desk. When it rang, Vernon was very quick to tell us it was probably his wife calling about the game results. He picked up the phone and the fun began. The conversation went something like this: "Why did you call me here? You know what I told you. I said if Chicago wins, do not call. You never listen to me when I tell you anything. Now I will fix it so you never call here on this phone again."

With this, he yanked the phone off the cradle, threw it on the floor, and then kicked it about twenty feet down the building. There was dead silence for an instant and then Clayton spoke. "Oh my god, what are we going to tell the boss?" By this time, I had realized that once again he had reeled us in, hook, line, and sinker. We all had a great laugh at this one and talked about it for weeks. We knew sooner or later there would be another episode like this one, but never sure when or where it would take place.

This story was one of the best. We were working the midnight shift again, and Vernon had gone to great pains of pulling this one off. He told all of us about this little caper except for one person, Matthew. (We called him Mattie.) Mattie was a fine gentleman and a very conscientious worker. He was also slightly afraid of the dark and probably believed in ghosts. Strange noises or anything out of the ordinary would have an unsettling effect on him. Vernon knew this and decided Mattie should be the star attraction for this show. We broke for lunch at 3:00 a.m. Everything was quiet at first as we were all eating and not ready to talk. From out of the blue came this soft voice, "Mattie, Mattie." The rest of us ignored the sound as we were all aware of the events to take place. Mattie looked around the lunch table at each one of us, but did not say a word. The voice sounded again.

"Mattie, are you there, Mattie?" It was so hard to keep our composure as we tried not to look at Mattie. This time, he spoke. "Did you guys hear that?" We assured him we heard nothing. More silence for a minute or two, and the strange voice appeared to sound a little louder. "Mattie, do you hear me? Talk to me, Mattie, I am in this lunch box and I need to get out." Once again, Mattie looked at each one of us and said, "Now I know you all heard that." We could not hold out any longer. We broke out into laughter and Mattie was still in awe as to what might be going on. Vernon went over to his own lunch box and took out his recorder that he had brought from home and showed it to Mattie. It was another chance for Mattie to laugh and shed a few tears. We would have a few more good years working together and certainly a lot of fun while doing so.

The Old Radio

This next little trick was related to me by Vernon, and it was played on one of his neighbors at home. It was a cleanup day, the day you can put out all sorts of rubble, old furniture, wooden boxes, old lamps, etc. Vernon was preparing a few things to go when he saw his neighbor drag out an old radio with a wooden case. It was in fair condition, but obviously did not work. He watched his elderly neighbor go in and out several times and timed each trip. He did this for a special reason. He went inside and found a little transistor radio. As his neighbor went inside his house, Vernon ran over and placed the little radio inside the old wooden one, turned it on, and ran back inside his own house and waited.

In a minute or two, the man's wife came out into the yard and stopped. She was listening to something. She called out to her husband. "Hey, John, come out here quick! That old radio is working." John came out, listened, and said to his wife, "I don't hear anything, and besides, the old radio is not even plugged in." She grabbed him by the hand and took him closer. Sure enough, he heard it. He looked into the old radio and started to laugh. He knew right away who had pulled this little trick. He also knew that they were being watched by Vernon even if he was not in sight.

Vernon passed away shortly after this, and we all felt a great loss. I can't speak for the others, but it was a loss that hurt me very deeply. He had a special way of lifting the burden off a lot of shoulders. He made me realize how important it is to search for the lighter side of every situation. He was kind enough to teach me how to play golf. He could point out my mistakes and at the same time make me laugh. He was taken from his family and friends much too early in life. I am sure that to this day, and far beyond our understanding, he is planning ways to make more people laugh.

I spent twelve years working at the Dartmouth office before I joined the staff at the district and regional level in Halifax. I have many fond memories of those early years in spite of the hard work and shift work. Christmastime was especially difficult due to the tremendous increase in the volumes of mail. It was normal to work long hours each day and seldom have a full day off in December. Time with our families was limited, and by Christmas Day, we were too tired to enjoy the festivities. There were many workdays that were a lot of fun, however, in spite of the long hours.

As soon as the rush of mail started, the hiring of part-time help began. This was a fun time as there would be a lot of new faces and lots of excitement. Most of the part-time helpers were excellent workers and required very little supervision beyond the initial training. There were a few exceptions, and I will mention one. The last few years I worked there, I was a supervisor and had about six people working on the shift with me. During the Christmas season, that number would jump to about twenty to twenty-five. The full-time employees were all well trained and would look after regular mail. This left the supervisors to handle the larger number of part-time workers. There was never a dull moment. A lot of these people came back year after year and knew exactly what to do. There was very little need to worry about them. Some of the younger people, however, were a different story. I should point out, however, that given the proper training and showing them that they were there to work paid large dividends. When the Christmas season was over, there was not one of them that I would not rehire.

One young fellow was quite a handful at first. His father was employed with Canada Post as well and encouraged him to seek employment there. The young man did not want to work so he spent his first few hours goofing off and disrupting the others. When we were all busy trying to keep ahead of the workload, the floor would quite often become a mess of elastic bands. These elastic bands were used to tie the bundles of mail together. This young man decided to shoot a few of these at some young boys nearby. I caught him in the act and called him aside. I explained the danger of shooting these bands and told him I had a special job for him. I found a large cardboard box and made him go all over the main floor and pick up every rubber band he could see. The sorting cases were in rows with about three feet of space between the cases. His job was quite simple. He had to walk up and down each row and pick up all rubber bands. I approached another young friend of his and gave him a box filled with rubber bands. I told him to follow behind the first young boy and sprinkle the floor with the bands. Telling him to make sure he wasn't seen. After about an hour, the first boy came to me and said he could not get them all cleaned because as fast as he did, the floor would be covered again. I told him he had ten more minutes to try again. If he could not keep up, his work would be terminated. After telling him this, I approached the fellow who was dropping the elastic bands and asked him to end his little exercise and go back to his regular work. It was not long after that he approached me again to tell me he finally got the bands all cleaned up. He apologized to me for his previous actions and promised to do much better if I let him stay on the job. He became one of the better workers we had that season.

A few years later, I met the young gentleman and he thanked me again for giving him the second chance. He also thanked me for not telling his father.

The part-time employees worked eight hours a day. They had a lunch break and two coffee breaks each day. They were always very punctual and cooperative. There was one evening, however, when they decided to play a trick on me. It was near the end of the big rush of mail, and they would soon be finished for the season. I had told them to take their fifteen-minute break. One lady told me they had decided to come back when they were ready. I laughed and told them I did not care. After about twenty minutes, they were still not there. I strolled around casually for a few minutes to see if I might see them. How can a supervisor lose fifteen or twenty people? I discovered them hiding in the stairwell, but they did not know I saw them. Because there was not a lot of work to do, I decided to leave them there until they were ready to come out. They did not expect this, and as a matter of fact, they were worried that they would all lose their jobs. They came back very shortly and went to their work stations. I walked past them and said, "Well, you folks had a short break tonight." One little lady said she was so scared I would fire them all. They appreciated the flexibility I gave them and paid me back twofold. Overall, their work ethic was above reproach. It is amazing how much cooperation you can receive when you treat people with respect.

I will now move on to my little brother. It seems I have jumped from one time frame to another on more than one occasion. This is a reflection of the author and not a misprint.

My little brother was quite a few years younger than me so we did not get to spend a lot of time together. By the time he started school, I was almost finished high school so we were never in the same school together. We have in later years shared a lot of laughs, and I will relate one or two. When he was very young, he came up behind me on the living room couch with a metal sand bucket. I had not done anything to provoke the attack, but he hit me over the head with it. Now this will explain some of the weird things I do. Another thing he did as a small boy was throw a flashlight battery into the fireplace. No one knew he had done this, but we would soon hear the effects as the battery exploded and blew live coals and ashes onto the living room floor. It was not until all flames were extinguished and Father found the remains of the battery that the story was told by Dennis with tears in his eyes. Dennis has remained in the Musquodoboit Valley all his life, and I am proud that he did stay there. He owns the old home we shared, and it is always alive with beautiful plants and flowers, summer and winter.

I think most of us would have preferred to stay in the area we were born in, but it is hard to do, especially if you were born in the country.

Dennis and I shared a lot of good times with Aunt Fanny. I have mentioned her several times, and she deserved recognition. She was always so nice to us. I loved her stories even when she exaggerated just a little. Dennis also had an aunt Mae who was a wonderful lady and laughed at almost every occasion. She was a sister to Dennis's mother. You will note I like quotes, so here we go again.

The most wasted of all days is one without laughter.
(E. E. Cummings)

Dennis Burke Taylor 2010.

The Big Rubber Boots

Abig part of country living is being outdoors. To most, it means some sort of hard work. To the younger folks, it often means a number of fun things. When I was first married and our children were quite young (three boys—Corey, Kendall, and Joe), I was a grown man, but part of me wanted to remain a boy. I think I did everything that was expected of me, but I was reluctant to give in totally and adjust. One of the things I am most thankful for is the fact that I decided to stay a boy. To this day, I think young, and I hope to keep on doing so. The last thing we need is to become old people who sit around complaining about the younger generation.

I tried to spend a lot of time with the boys and give them as much attention as I could. I made it a point to try to become their friend, as well as their dad. This is not an easy task no matter how much fun it can be. When you are a parent, there are lines you should not cross. I feel that growing children need their space, as well as guidance. I remember my father giving me guidance on several occasions, and I was not even aware he was doing it. I would talk to him, ask a question or two, and listen while he talked to me. In the course of our conversation, the answer would come to me. He had a way of steering me in the right direction and making it seem like it was my idea. I never realized how he did this, but I always wanted to do the same for my own boys. Sometimes it is best to be a good listener and let them vent their frustrations. In doing this, they will find their own solutions. I am certainly not an expert, but I do know this: you become a parent as soon as your first child is born. Being a good parent is a continuing process. If you succeed, the rewards are unlimited.

We spent many hours at the hockey rinks, baseball fields, etc., and every hour was pure joy for me. We went camping on many occasions, but I am not sure they always got the full enjoyment that was planned for them. Oh, we had a few great trips, and I was probably the happiest camper. At a recent gathering, one of the boys said, "We want to take you and Mom out camping some weekend in the rain." It became all too clear to me that some of the trips we had were not as much fun as I had envisioned. I worked shift work at that time, and weekends off were scarce. I had one long weekend in every four. I made plans to camp on those occasions, and rain did not deter me.

Later, when I bought property and started to build a cottage, the boys were there in force to help out. I guess the thought of rain on a solid roof was much better than rain on a canvas tent. They were good years, and I enjoyed their company to the fullest, rain or shine. We should embrace the younger people and connect with them as often as we can. The boys are all married now with families of their own, and so the cycle goes on. I am the granddad now and still want to be a boy.

When the boys were quite young, I agreed to help my father-in-law rebuild an old hunting camp he had built several years before. It was first designed to go on the back of his three-ton Dodge truck. He wanted to put it on a permanent spot. He owned a woodlot in Dean and wanted to have a place to stay at night when he was working there. The work went well, and soon the new camp was ready for guests. There would soon be many visits to this camp by young and old. It is still there, but vacancies are all taken up by the mice. My brother-in-law Freeman Dean and I spent more than a few memorable trips there. On one occasion, Freeman had a friend, Harvey, who had never spent a night in a camp and certainly not one in the woods and who asked if we would take him along. He said he always wanted to do this. We decided to take him for the night and loaded up the old tractor with supplies, and off we went. Harvey was in a new world. He was older than we were but acted like a young lad when we were on our way. He was doing great until darkness came upon us and then the fear replaced the fun.

We had an oil lamp and a good stove to keep us warm, but the little noises outside got his attention. He began to settle down just before we decided to go to bed, but fear would soon come rushing back. Several months before this adventure, we had lined most of the inside boards with old flattened-out cardboard boxes. It helped keep out some of the cold when the fire died down. Shortly after we settled down for the night and lights were out, Freeman reached toward the wall and scratched the cardboard. The sound was eerie, but I knew right away what had happened. Harvey had no idea what it was, but sleep was not on his agenda for the rest of the night. As soon as morning arrived, Harvey was ready to head back to the open country and never again spend a night in the woods. The old camp became a great place to visit for many people, and soon after this, another boy wanted to join us on one of our visits. He was about twelve years old and from a large family, so going to a camp in the woods was a real treat for him. He was my wife's cousin and lived handy her parent's home. He was always hanging around his older cousin Freeman and worshipped the ground he walked on. We agreed to take him along to help out with the chores around the camp. He was delighted to go and was a delight to have along. Unlike the older guest, Harvey, who had been with us just before, this young man was not afraid of the dark.

This trip was a real adventure. We arrived at the camp just before dark. We forgot to take matches with us and managed to find just one match in the camp. Being very careful, we got the oil lamp lit, only to discover the lamp was very low on oil. We made a fire in the old woodstove, but soon realized that if the stove and lamp both went out in the night, we were going to be cold and hungry the next day.

I remembered an old abandoned camp less than a half mile down the river and decided to go look for more matches and perhaps some lamp oil. I did have one flashlight and got ready to set out. The other two boys decided it would be fun to go along, even if it was pitch-dark. The old cabin we were in was beside the river, and the old abandoned one was down the old road alongside the river. The old road was very rough and had large rocks and water almost everywhere. We all had the proper footwear, big rubber boots. The smaller boy had boots that were much too big for him but slopped along with the greatest of ease. We were about halfway there when we came upon a long water puddle with rocks scattered along the road. I had the only flashlight so I went across first, being careful to walk on each rock. When I got over the worst part, I held the light for our little friend Lyle. He was doing quite well as I held the light on each rock and he stepped from one to the other. Just as he jumped to the last rock, I somehow lost my concentration and moved the light. I heard a little yelp and a big splash. When I moved the light, he was in motion and had no idea where he was going to land. This was many years ago, and I don't remember if I did it on purpose or if it was an accident. I think it was an accident, but I will let my readers decide.

We soon got him up, dried him off a little, then continued on our quest for needed supplies. We were very fortunate as there were matches and oil both in the old run-down camp. We hurried back to our cozy cabin, got our good friend dried off and in warm clothes. We hung his big boots up to dry over the stove. The three of us had a great laugh over this incident and settled in for a great trip. We would meet again several years later and continue our laugh.

There was another occasion later on that created a lot of concern and in the end much more laughter. It was during a weekend visit to Dean to help my father-in-law cut wood for the coming winter. It was early spring, and there was still several inches of snow left on the ground. We were using the old camp as a shelter from the elements and to eat our lunch that day. Just before lunch, we started to cut down an old maple tree. Geordie, my father-in-law, had cut the tree through with the chain saw, but it hung up on another tree. It was still about six or eight feet from the ground. I told him I would walk up the tree and perhaps my weight would bring it down. He decided to walk up closer to the treetop and pull one of the larger branches down. He did this, and with my weight, the tree came right to the ground. I heard him shout, "Oh my god, my teeth!" I looked his way, expecting to see blood flowing from his mouth. He seemed to be okay, but he was bent over looking down. When I got closer to him, I found him digging in the snow with his hands. I asked him what happened and his reply was, "One of the limbs ripped the pocket off my shirt and my teeth fell into the snow." I was not much help as I was laughing so hard that tears were clouding my eyes. He did find the teeth, and this time he held them very securely.

When we broke for lunch, he cleaned his teeth, and this time he put them in his mouth. We had many laughs about this later. I had never met a man who laughed more than he did. There was another time we were in the woods with Geordie and his son Freeman, and we went to do some rabbit hunting. The plan was to walk along the road that passed our camp and continue on right back to the end of the property. This would be almost a mile. We had walked about halfway when Geordie told us he had an important chore to do and we should walk slow until he caught up to us. He headed into the woods on the side of the road. The trees were very close together and quite small. We decided to wait right there for a short while. Freeman decided to get down on his knees and look into the woods where his father had gone. Sure enough, he saw him bent over with his pants down and his back to us. The snow was soft and damp, just right for a snowball. Freeman quickly made one and threw it toward his father. His aim was perfect as the ball bounced a few times and then hit the target. It landed right where his pants would normally be. We heard an unkind oath and decided it would be best for us to leave the scene as quickly as possible.

We walked a long distance and then waited for him to come along. He never mentioned the incident, and we did not let on that we knew what had happened. We were not sure if he knew what really hit him and decided it was best to continue on our hunting trip. I don't remember shooting any rabbits that day, and that is a good thing. The snowball was enough excitement for one day.

My brother-in-law Freeman passed away on September 11, 2013, one day short of his sixty-eighth birthday. He was not only my brother-in-law, but he was also one of my best friends. We shared a lot of good times and sure did our share of laughing. In the early years just after his sister Vivian and I got married, he would rely on me for help with special projects. There were far too many to mention in one chapter, but I will relate a few of the most important. I think the model plane experience would rate quite high. I had bought myself a Piper Cub kit and carefully put it together. It was one with balsa wood, paper, paint, and other bare essentials.

When Freeman saw this, he decided he was going to have one and he would also purchase an engine and fly it as well. I helped him put the plane together. Like mine, it was bright yellow and a thing of beauty. He had ordered his engine and waited for days before it arrived. When he finally received it, he could not wait for the weekend to come so I would come from the city to help him install the engine. When that time arrived, he was all pumped up and ready to fly. We had the new engine and all the essentials to make it fly. I suggested he should check the engine before we attached it to the plane. He did this by placing the motor in a vise down in his dad's garage. After a successful start-up, the engine worked just fine.

Now he was ready for the real test flight. We mounted the engine in its proper place at the front of the aircraft. I suggested he should first secure some kind of line to the plane to give him at least a little control.

He said there was no need for this as he would only put a small amount of fuel in the little tank. His theory was, when the plane ran out of fuel, it would slowly glide to the grass in the direction the plane would be going (not necessarily so). The first flight was to start in the garage and then fly straight out through the garage door. He held the plane while I started the motor. In an instant, it flew out the garage door just like he said it would, but rapidly gained altitude, so much so that we lost sight of the plane. We heard the whine of the engine as it flew almost straight up. Before we could get out of the garage to see it, the noise ceased, and the plane came to a sudden crash about fifteen feet in front of us in the driveway. The plane was a wreck, and so was the motor. We should have cried, but not Freeman; he laughed so hard at the whole episode. We both talked about it later on, but that was the last of our model flying. We were never anything like the Wright brothers.

A year or two before the model plane incident, Freeman asked me to help him make a kite. I had tried a few times before to build one for myself but could never get one off the ground. I agreed to give it another go. We got all the supplies together and actually put one together that had some potential. After a long period of time, we discovered that it would fly quite well as long as it was gaining altitude. When the kite came to the end of the string, it would dart from side to side and quickly return to earth. We did not have a lot of string so I suggested he get his fishing rod and reel. It was a small one and quite light. He did this, and it really worked. It went much farther up and seemed to fly really well. Freeman kept releasing the line a little at a time, and it went higher and higher. The wind was quite strong but steady. Then his line came to an end and the kite started to dive again. The wind gave a sudden gust, causing a strong pull on the kite. Before he realized what had happened, the kite was gone along with his fishing pole. The flight continued unmanned up the hill behind the house and finally snagged a tall tree well into the woods.

We followed the flight trail up to the woods and retrieved the fishing pole that was swinging on a branch just off the ground. The kite was well lodged at the top of a huge spruce tree, and perhaps it is still there.

There was another experiment that Freeman tried on his own before I arrived on the scene. I did not witness it, but he told me about it later on. He had found an old pair of skis at his aunt's house and asked if he could take them home. He had an excellent hill behind his parents' house and made several trips down this hill, and each time, he got better at it. Then he got the idea that he would like to make a ski jump. He found an old wooden door that would make an excellent ramp. He placed it about halfway down the hill with the lower end lifted enough to give him the desired liftoff. He covered the upper end with snow and packed it down. The rest of the door he neglected to cover with snow. Now for his trial run. He came down the hill like a pro and went over the ramp flying. The landing was not that smooth, however. When his skis hit the old door, they stuck to the wood, and he continued on without his skis. He landed face-first in the packed snow. Helmets and goggles were not heard of at that time, so needless to say, his face took the force. His glasses were broken, I believe, and no doubt he had some bruises. I believe that was also the end of his skiing career. He would tell this story quite often and always had a good laugh at his own expense. He was a friend to all. And we miss him dearly. We shared a lot of good times over the years, and the memories will always be with me.

Everyone should spend a night in a camp like this.

The Outhouse Door

Sometimes the strangest circumstances will cause the most enjoyment. During our early cottage days at Melmerby Beach, we had the bare essentials and made do with what we could provide. Indoor plumbing did not come until later years. We were fortunate that we were not used to a lot of comforts in our early age and did not mind the old privy as long as it was clean. My brother Keith and his wife Joan would come down quite often to camp with us and quite often brought their youngest son Brian along to enjoy the beach and, of course, be entertained by his father and uncle Robert. My wife Vivian and our three sons Corey, Kendall, and Joe came along many times as well.

Sometime during one of these weekends at the beach, my nephew Brian (about ten years old) decided it would be fun to lock me in the outhouse, and with the aid of my son Joe, they formalized a plan. It was not a difficult plan. They just had to keep an eye out for me and wait until I felt the need to visit the john. The latch on the door was the old style that protruded through the door. There was a locking device on the outside of the door and a hook inside to keep others out. If ever there was a need to lock the outside, there was a built-in hole in the latch where a stick or any suitable piece of material could be used to secure the door.

After finding an opportunity to lock me in for the first time and listening to my complaints, it became a regular thing for Brian. My son Joe had given up the ritual as I think he knew my limits and also knew he did not want to be on the receiving end of anything I might do to them. He did, however, stay close enough to watch the show.

My nephew Brian got a big thrill by doing this several times. He would place a small stick in the latch, and as I tried to exit, I would have to push the door hard enough to break the stick. He would always be close enough to hear me, but not close enough to be caught. One day, I told him I had devised a method of getting even with him. When he asked me what it was, I said, "One day you will find out." I went along with his practice of trying to lock me in for several times during the summer.

Finally, I decided it was time to put my plan in place. I found a nice piece of pine, two inches by one inch and about three feet long. I hid this in the privy and waited for my chance. Now I want to explain something very important. I was not mad at my nephew for his little antics, and I would never cause him any physical harm. I just felt it was time to let him know what could happen to him.

When the next lock-in occurred, I was ready. I knew he had placed the small stick in the latch. I located the stick I had hidden and shoved it down the hole, into the brown stuff to a depth of about eight inches. I was careful when I withdrew my pine stick with the brown end. Brian was watching me from a distance as he always did, only this time he had a very strange look on his face. I broke the door open with the stick in my hand. I ran after him as soon as I put one foot out the door. He took off like a scalded cat toward the beach road. Brian was not noted for his speed on foot, but this day, he would set a record. I had never considered touching him with this stick or doing him any harm, but he did not know this at the time.

I chased him for several yards at full speed and then I returned to the cottage. He did not return for about twenty minutes, and even then, he came back very cautiously, making sure I was not in hiding and ready to start the chase once more. He gave up his little habit with the privy door, but we had several occasions to laugh about it later.

In later years, he got married and invited our family to the wedding and reception. Finding him a suitable wedding gift was easy for me. I found a pine stick exactly like the one I had in the privy. This time, I coated about eight inches of the stick with brown silicone and let it dry well. No one else would help me so I wrapped his gift myself and presented it to him during their gift-opening party. I watched as he carefully opened the package. As soon as he saw the brown end of the stick, he quickly put the package under the table. To the best of my knowledge, it has never been seen since.

I have not seen Brian very often lately, but we will both remember those good days.

A Fishy Car

Not long after I finished high school, I went to Toronto, Ontario, to make my first million. That was not really my objective, nor did I ever achieve it, but it was a great experience. The boy from the country lands in downtown Toronto, and soon I was strolling along Danforth Avenue and within days had a good job. At that time, finding a job was easy, especially if you came from the Maritimes.

Most employers found the people from the Maritimes the best workers. One of my first requirements was a car. I found a good deal right away, a 1950 Austin sedan. What a treasure I thought it was. I later found out that it was not the best car in the world, but I did have a lot of happy miles in it, and it was mine. Not long after I purchased the car, I came home again and drove my little car all the way. I will never forget that trip. I left Toronto on February 14, 1957. It was a three-day journey and a very cold one at that. My sister Frances packed enough lunch to last me all the way home.

I stayed in motels on two occasions. The first night cost me $6.50, and the second was $7.00. My total gas bill for the trip was $19.50. I mention this part as it is leading up to some other fun we had with the old Austin. Soon after I arrived home, I got a job working in a bank in Truro (I did not make my million there either). While I worked there, I stayed in Truro on weekdays and traveled to the Musquodoboit Valley on most weekends.

It was one of those weekends that I parked my little car at a friend's place and went to a dance in Elderbank on a Saturday night. I don't remember too much about the dance that night, but I do remember that the ladies all went home with someone else. My friend and I got back to his place, and I was soon in my little car and on my way to my dad's house to spend the night. Along the way, I could smell a strange smell in the car. It was an odor that was not a normal one for my dear little car. It was too late to do an examination that night, so I was up early in the morning to search. It did not take long in daylight. I lifted the engine bonnet and found several Gaspereaux baked on my engine manifold. One or more of my best buddies had placed them there for my enjoyment while I was at the dance. When I searched further, I found several under the seat and one in the glove compartment.

I was not pleased, but I knew that no real harm had been done and I would find out who the culprits were eventually. To my sorrow, however, the smell in the car seemed to get worse as the days went by. I searched every little nook I could find and still no luck. It was about two weeks before I discovered the source of my problems. In the center of the rear seat was a pullout armrest. It was for the comfort of those who were seated in the back. When I opened the armrest, the smell was enough to make one sick. The one lonely fish had been there for weeks and had decayed to the point of mush. I am sure when I finally traded the car, the smell was still there or at least I imagined so.

It was not too long before the word leaked out and I found the ones who had given me the fish fry. There would be no doubt they had a great laugh. From then on, it was a plan to return the favor. When something like this happens, it is not always wise to get even right away. It is far more interesting if you just bide your time and watch your friends get more and more nervous. The ones who went fishing and left half their catch in my car knew me well. They knew it was only a matter of time and I would be on their trail.

I eventually had the opportunity to get even, but I must admit it was not anything original. It was on a Saturday night again, and you guessed it, we were off to the Elderbank dance. On this occasion, I had three other guys with me, and there were at least two other cars going to the dance as well. One of the boys who pulled the fish trick on me parked his pickup at a local service station and went along with another friend.

My accomplice and I knew the time was right. We put our plan to work right away. The dance would have to wait a few minutes. Like I said, it was not an original idea, but we sure provided a lot of laughs later on. We had a jack in the car so we used it to lift Aubrey's truck off the rear wheels. We were careful to lift it just far enough to get the wheels barely off the ground. We placed wooden blocks under the axle just inside the wheel hubs then let the jack down with the axle on the blocks. That was all we had to do and then we were off to the dance.

When the dance was over, we made sure we left in time to see the events to follow. We also mentioned it to several of our friends. When Aubrey arrived to pick up his truck, there were several people hiding in the bushes nearby to watch the show. I want you to know Aubrey was one of my best friends, and we would laugh about these events many times later on.

He did not waste any time getting into his truck and had it started right away. He revved the motor and let out the clutch. Nothing moved. We were all close enough to see his face and watch his expressions. He got

out and walked around the truck then got back in to try it again. It still would not move. He got out and checked under the hood— nothing he could see. Got back in and tried again. Each time, he looked more worried. The people who were enjoying the show were doing their best to hold back the laughter.

Finally, the light went on, and he scrambled out with a big smile on his face. Got his jack out and in a few minutes was ready to head home. We broke the silence with laughter, along with him. I told him later that this trick was just a sample because his trick on me had more lasting effects. I just wanted him to be looking over his shoulder for a long, long time.

There was another trip with the old car that was very eventful as well. It was back in Toronto. A very good friend of mine, Richard Price, came up from Nova Scotia to work and boarded with my sister Thelma and her family. We had been good friends for a few years as we went to school together. A few months after he arrived, my sister and family moved to Sutton, Ontario, where my brother-in-law had gone to work. Richard and I remained in Toronto and started boarding with Frances, another sister of mine.

On most weekends, we would drive to Sutton as it was much more like home. It was a quiet country town. I had purchased my little car before this so we used it to travel back and forth. On one of our trips, the car started to give us problems. It would stall or just slow down to a ridiculous pace when we needed more speed for the hills. We had just started out of Toronto on the Old Don Valley road when it stalled first. We were almost to the top of the hill coming up out of the valley. When it stalled on us, it would not start with the starter. With the gear ratio it had in reverse, we could not coast backward to start it, so we would have to turn it around and run down the hill to hopefully get it going. In order to do this, I would back it around as far as I could on the hill and Richard (Dick) would jump out and push it forward down the hill. The plan was simple. I would leave him to walk farther up the hill, and I would go all the way down to the bottom, turn around, and go up as fast as I could. Each time, I got up farther, but each time the car would quit on me. We decided to give it one final try. We were to follow the same pattern. We got the car turned, and I started to roll down the hill. Just as I did this, Dick decided he would jump in. I saw what he was trying to do so I put the brakes on. I did this just as he opened the door to get in. He was running, and as I put the brakes on, his momentum thrust him in headfirst and right under the dash.

It was dark by this time, but a very quick check gave both of us assurance that he was fine. Down to the bottom of the hill we went, turned around, put on full throttle, and sailed over the top. We had several miles to go, but it was all quite level from then on. After traveling a few miles, Dick said his face was all wet. I turned on the inside lights to see blood all over his right eye. One more stop to get some snow from the side of the road to cool him down. We continued to our destination, and my sister Thelma soon had him cleaned up and as good as new. A short time later, Dick got his own car and also started working in Sutton. We were proud of our little cars and spent a lot of time traveling the snowy roads on the outskirts of this beautiful town. This reminds me of a gentleman from Upper Musquodoboit, who was leaving home to look for work. His objective, as he told it, was, "I am going to work long enough to get a car, then I am going to come home again just long enough to pass everyone who ever passed me and splash everyone who ever splashed me."

In the years gone by, there were a lot of dirt roads. In wet weather, there were always puddles of water on the road. It was a total insult to pedestrians to get splashed by vehicles going by. Most drivers were very considerate and slowed down to prevent this. There were other drivers who had very little concern and became the victims of harsh reprimands, even if they did not hear it from the poor people who were splashed with muddy water.

In September of 2013, I had an opportunity to visit the old house on Milverton Boulevard in Toronto where I stayed in 1956. I even got to walk up the street where I drove my very first car home. What a thrill it was to go back in time.

This trip brought back memories of working with my brother-in-law Victor Flemming. I had a full-time job with Dunlop Tire, but I worked on Saturdays to help Victor. He had a job with Botnick's Furniture Store in downtown Toronto. We spent most of our time delivering furniture. One morning when we arrived, there was a huge chesterfield waiting for delivery. A gentleman came in Friday evening, decided he liked it, paid for it, and asked to have it delivered early in the morning. The delivery was about six blocks away in an old apartment building. When we arrived, we learned that it was up three long flights of stairs. Now Victor was a strong man, but I only weighed 130 pounds and I was anything but strong. We worked at it and managed to get it delivered. The man who bought it looked at it from all angles and finally said, "I don't care for the color. I think I would like you guys to take it back."

Victor looked at the guy for a few seconds and then replied, "I think you should get used to the color because we are not taking it back." That was the end of the transaction, and nothing more was ever said. I guess he learned to like his new furniture.

We had a similar experience on another delivery a few hours later. We were delivering a rather large chesterfield to another old rooming house just off King Street. We had to go up one flight of stairs for this one (piece of cake). When we got up the stairs and into the room he directed us to, we discovered that the room was so small there was not a single wall wide enough for the piece of furniture. The man was not disturbed and said just put it from corner to corner. There were two lamps that went with the chesterfield. When we looked for a wall plug to plug them in, he informed us that there were no plugs in that room. The situation was becoming rather strange, and we were having a laugh. He told us there was a plug in his other room, which served as a kitchen and Lord knows what else. We both looked in the room and found a wall plug on the wall between his new chesterfield and kitchen. Victor told him he would need a long cord to go around. He had a better idea. He grabbed a hammer

137

and smashed a hole in the wall on both sides and put the lamp cord through, plugged it in, and said, "Let there be light!"

Several years after that, I had an opportunity to visit Victor and my sister Thelma at their cottage in Bancroft, Ontario.

I had been working in Ottawa and stopped in for the weekend on my way home. It turned out to be a fun family weekend. My sister Frances and my brother-in-law Glen also had a cottage there, and we were to do a few chores. Victor had a wharf that went out into the small lake. It was supported by four plastic barrels that were under the platform of the wharf. One of the barrels had somehow been cracked and was no longer of any use. Glen arrived with a new barrel and said we should get that little chore done right away. Glen was not one to take part in any of the water sports but agreed to help with this little repair if he did not have to go into the water. Victor and I put on some swimming gear and braved the cool water while Glen stayed up on the wharf. We had to push the new barrel down underneath the edge of the wharf. This was difficult as the water was too deep for us to stand on the bottom. We came upon a great idea. Victor and I would hold the barrel in place, and Glen could push it down under the wharf. He got down on his knees just at the edge and put his hands on the side of the barrel. We decided we would all push at the count of three. The barrel went down under so quickly that Glen lost his balance and went into the water headfirst. We both reached out to rescue him. In no time, he was in and dressed in warm clothing. We all relived that moment many times over.

A few years later, in 1985, I was assigned a teaching position in Ottawa, Ontario. It was a short-term position during the winter months. I never considered myself a teacher, but this was a special opportunity for me. I was only able to come home every third weekend so I made it a point to visit family in Bancroft, Ontario, on the weekends I was not going home. My sister Thelma was sick at the time so I was able to spend some valuable time with her. Bancroft is a beautiful little town, and in the winter, the snowmobiling was great. My brothers-in-law Victor and Glen had several machines so I got to travel several miles each time I visited. We had so many good times. On one occasion, they took me on a long run over several lakes and hills around the area. The weather was nice, but it was cloudy. As we were traveling along one trail, Victor, who had been leading, waved Glen to take the lead. A few minutes later, we stopped for a rest. Glen came over to me and whispered, "Victor will only let you lead when he does not know where he is going." While we were taking our break, I looked through the trees and thought I could see a glimpse of the sun. I told them what I saw, but Victor told me the sun would have to be on the other side as we were going north. In just a few minutes, the sun came out in all its splendor right where I had thought I had seen it. Nothing more was said, but the machines were turned around and we headed north and were soon home. While there, I ended the evenings visiting with our sister. She passed away that summer.

It was very difficult to leave when I visited that winter as I never knew if I would see her again. I am very thankful, however, that my work took me to that area when it did. Thelma was eight years older than me, but it never showed. In spite of her poor health in later years, she maintained her sense of humor and laughed more than most people with excellent health.

Several years prior to this, Thelma and my sister Mildred were sent to the school for the blind in Halifax. This all came about because of an overzealous teacher. As it turned out, Thelma did have serious sight problems, which were dealt with in haste, but Mildred's eyes were fine. She was dyslexic. I heard about this from my father in later years. I had driven him to Halifax to visit a friend in the hospital. As we were parking, he saw the old school for the blind building. He started to cry but tried to hide it. When I asked him about it, he told me all about his trip from Upper Musquodoboit to Halifax on the train. He had to bring his girls in and leave them. After a few long weeks, the ordeal was over and his family came back home. Thelma did have problems with her eyes for the rest of her life, but she continued to cope very well. After she moved to Toronto, she went to work at the institute for the blind and worked there for many years. Every day for her was a positive experience.

Mildred came home with new glasses as well, but that was not her problem. After several productive years, she died of cancer. Her strong points were many, but her memory had to be on the top of her list. She was the family memory bank. I firmly believe that when you lose people close to you, part of them stays with you to help you become a better person.

Now on a lighter note. Have you ever noticed that as we grow older, we gain much more knowledge, but the people around us pay less and less attention? Think about it.

Grandfather's Car the Malibu

My father had a heart attack when he was in his midsixties and was forced to quit work. Just prior to his heart problems, he had purchased a new 1966 Chevrolet Malibu and had driven it very little. It sat in his yard most of the time, and although the power train was very good, the body began to rust quite rapidly.

When my oldest son Corey finished high school, he went on to community college to study heavy-duty mechanics. He could not travel on the school bus any longer, so transportation would become a major problem. At that time, my wife and I had a hard time keeping one vehicle on the road, and buying a second one was not in our future plans. My father came up with a solution. We were visiting there one weekend, and Corey was looking at the Malibu in the yard that had not been driven in a long time. Father saw him from the kitchen window and went out to talk to him. I could not hear the conversation so I could only watch as the two of them walked around the car several times. A short time later, they came in to announce that Corey had a car to go to school in.

I was very appreciative of the gift, but I was also afraid. I could just see this car going with metal parts falling off it at every bump in the road. Corey was so excited it more than made up for any fear I had. He soon got the car tied together in fine fashion, and they went to school in it for several months. He spent many hours tinkering with it and keeping it in the best shape he could. I am sure it served him and his friends well and went places a father should not know about.

There is a fun story I will tell you about Corey and his car, but first, I should mention my father and one of his driving habits. My father never filled his gas tank unless he was planning a very long trip. He used his vehicles to go to and from his work throughout the Musquodoboit Valley. During the years, somewhere between 1945 and 1980, two dollars' worth of gas would have been the norm. He carried almost every tool he had in his vehicle. Because he was a plumber, he always had a one-gallon can of naphtha gas with him. He had this to use in his blowtorch, but quite frequently, he would run out of gas in his vehicle and used some of the naphtha gas to get him home. You can verify this by talking to my brothers. They would laugh and say it was true. I have been with him several times when this happened and would tell him he should simply put more gas in his car. He would laugh and say, "Yes, I should."

It was on a very cold windy night that I got a call from Corey telling me he was stranded at a shopping plaza. He had run out of gas. I got a can of gas and went to rescue him. He was cold and frustrated and told me, "Dad, I will never run out of gas again." I consoled him the best I could and told him it was not the first time that had happened to the Malibu. I don't remember how many years the car lasted, but I do know that one of our relatives bought the motor and I think the agreement was they had to take what was left of the body.

It was a great gift to my son, and I know he appreciated it. My father never had a lot of money, but he was very generous. It was a very rare occasion that any of us went there without bringing something home. There were a number of times when I was in high school that he would come to me and hand me a dollar or two. I knew he was doing without something himself to help me along. I am sorry I never told him how grateful I was. I remember the day I left home to find work in Toronto. I had just turned eighteen. I was traveling with my sister Frances and her husband Glen. As we were leaving my dad's house, he reached out and put a ten-dollar bill in my hand. It was rolled up so no one else would know what it was. It might seem like a small amount, but it was more than he could afford. We both shed a tear, but we also tried to hide it. If I could go back in time, I would certainly tell him just how much he meant to me.

I was blessed with three sons, and each of them has made me very proud in their own special way. I hope I have been able to show them just how much I care for them.

To be in your children's memories tomorrow, you must be in their lives today. (Unknown)

Those who bring sunshine to others cannot keep it from themselves. (James M. Barrie)

The Great Train Rides

Ever since my early years, I have loved the trains. There is something so relaxing about them. For several years, I watched the old trains go past our home by the Cariboo Road in Upper Musquodoboit. I wanted to jump on and go along, but that did not happen until several years later.

I had trips to Montreal and Ottawa, and later a great trip through the Rockies, in the eighties. In April 2007, I went to Ontario with two of my brothers, Stewart and Keith. Keith had lost his wife, Joan, a few months before this, and we felt a trip would be good for him. As things turned out, it was good for all of us. We had so much fun that we decided right away we would go again the next year. Stewart's wife Kaye was not feeling well enough to travel at that time, but some of their family agreed to stay with her until Stewart returned.

The first year we traveled, we had a triple compartment. Stewart was the oldest so he got first pick of the bunks. He chose the one closest to the floor and running lengthwise with the train. I got to sleep in the upper bunk without a window. Keith had a bunk on the floor as well, but his was crossways with the train. When Keith lay down, his face was only a few inches from Stewart's feet (not a good idea). One of our main reasons for going was to surprise our sister Frances. We had several relatives there, but she was our main reason for going. We went by train to Belleville, Ontario, then rented a car. I had taken my GPS from home so we could map our way. When we picked up the car, Stewart got in the front seat with me. Brother Keith was relegated to the rear. Stewart was amused with the GPS and could not wait to see it in action.

I had it set for Ajax and started out onto the highway. The kind lady told me to turn right at the next street. Stewart said the lady was wrong and that we had to turn left. Keith started to laugh and said to Stewart, "You wanted to sit in front and be the navigator, and you couldn't even get the first turn right." Stewart was amused and surprised when he saw we actually were going the right way. He studied the GPS for quite a while and then said, "I should have one of these at home so that when I go to town, I will have someone to talk to me." On to Ajax, Ontario, where we were to stop and visit our niece Reta and her husband Peter. Our sister Frances and her husband Glen were on their way from Scarborough. Reta had invited her parents out for supper but did not tell her mother that three of her brothers would be there. We arrived just ahead of our sister and hid in the basement. We were relaxing in their rec room when they arrived. Frances was never one to get overly excited, but that evening, she was excited and had a tear or two for sure.

We left there the next day and drove toward Bancroft. On our way to Bancroft, Stewart, Keith, and I decided to tour a little on the way and stop for supper before we arrived at the cottage. In the village of Madoc, we found a little restaurant that had seen better days, but we were hungry and the food outlets were few and far between. We had a great dinner but decided to skip dessert. Just as we were about to leave, our waitress came and told us she had just taken a bread pudding out of the oven. The two of them got so excited they told me we had to stay for that. Just as we were ready to leave, Keith said he had to visit the little boys' room. After he left, Stewart told me he was paying this time so he went and paid the bill. He talked to the waitress for a few minutes and then filled me in on his plan. He had convinced the waitress to help him pull a little joke on brother Keith. She had agreed to claim that we were going out without paying.

When Keith did come past the door, she screamed at him as he touched the outside door, "Hey, you get back here and pay that bill! Who do you think you are running out without paying?" By this time, Stewart and I were just outside the door and trying to be serious. He swore he would find a way to get even.

Later, we met Frances and Glen again at their cottage. This was the start of a visit that will be forever lodged in our hearts. We played tricks on one another, and I learned so much about my older siblings. During the day, we traveled around the area and the evenings were filled with more stories. Our brother-in-law Victor Fleming also lived there close by. Our sister Thelma had passed away a few years before. It was a great chance for us to visit him as well. Our brother Malcolm also lived in

Bancroft after he retired from the air force. Unfortunately, he died of cancer before we made our trips. We made two more trips by train to visit. Stewart did not make the third trip, and we missed him. He is a wealth of information. Most of it is probably not important but funny. It was a wonderful opportunity for us to get together and bond a little more. When you are young, a few years between you and your siblings seems like a wide gap. After you get older, you seem closer to the same age. I think we were always a close family, but quite often, long distances kept us apart, but we did keep in touch.

Music in My Life

During the mideighties, my life changed dramatically. I became very interested in music. I had always liked music, but something happened to me that turned me toward playing. My father was a good fiddle player, but he hardly ever played. I remember that friends of his would try to get him to play, but he almost always refused. One day, he told us that the first one of us who learned to play would get his fiddle. I decided I would give it a try. I asked if I could take his fiddle home and get it in good playing condition and he agreed.

I was successful and got the fiddle in good shape. I enrolled in a group class for violin, and the very first night, I was playing my first tune. My work took me to Ottawa that winter, and I could not finish my lessons. However, the violin went with me, and every night I tried to play something that others would recognize. I did not tell my father that I was learning to play. I decided I would learn "Silent Night" and play it for him at Christmas. I did get to do that, and he cried when I played. At first, I thought my playing must be real bad if it made him cry, but his tears were tears of joy. He soon let me know that his fiddle was now in my hands to do as I saw fit.

From that day on, I was on a journey I grew to love. I must point out that I am not an accomplished player, but I enjoy doing the best I can. Over the past several years, I have met many wonderful people I would not have met if I had not started to play my dad's fiddle. There is an endless number of people who have touched my life since I learned that first tune. I have been very fortunate to have a lot of support from many other players, and I will be forever grateful.

The greatest reward has been watching people dance while our band plays. There have been times when we played for over two hundred people and all of them would dance. The smiles and laughter will always be remembered. Many times we have played for seniors, and each time it is more rewarding. Some of the people are hardly able to move but come to life when they hear the music. What a wonderful feeling to realize that such a small effort can give giant rewards.

Life may not be the party we hoped for, but while we are here, we should dance.

The Downhill Slide

As I start the last part of our book, I can't help but think I am on my way downhill. If I am, I should find it much easier to go anywhere I want to go. I am looking forward to it. I realize that aging is inevitable, but I have not seen a single reason for me to act any different than I did in my early years. I can still go places. I just take a little more time and enjoy the scenery along the way. They say we should stop and smell the roses. I have learned to do that. It really works. I try to listen more and talk less (having trouble with that one). During my working years, I changed from a very quiet person to one who talks most of the time. This all came about after I began working in sales and marketing. A lot of study and a boost of self-confidence have made a world of difference. So what if I am on my way downhill? I can still enjoy that method of travel.

I remember when I was just a child I thought that anyone over thirty was really old. Now all of my children are older than that. I don't think age is any more than a number. The rest is attitude. As long as I have a small measure of good health, I will continue to be a boy.

My main purpose for writing these stories was to give my family, many relatives, and all my friends a little insight into the life of this country boy. When I was growing up, I loved to listen to my dad and his friends talk about the hard times and the good times they had. I wish I had taken the time to write down so many things that are now lost. They would talk and laugh and I would listen. I loved the stories about the woods camps. They were my favorite. There were many cold winter nights when I would have my ears wide open even if it was long after I was supposed to be asleep. I did not want to miss a word. I wish we could take a break for just an hour once in a while—no television, computer, cell phone, or any other electronic gadget. Just one whole hour to listen to an old codger like myself tell a few stories. When we listen to stories, we not only hear, but we also have a picture in our mind that no one else can see. I remember when we were small and we got a chance to listen to the radio for a few minutes. Sometimes it would be *Boston Blackie, The Shadow, The Lone Ranger,* or one of many others we listened to. We all had a picture in our mind that was so real. I think television took the suspense out of a lot of these shows.

One of the most exciting times I ever had was listening to my grandfather Corey Taylor talk about his long walk along the Labrador coast and on into Quebec. He started at Dave Brook, Labrador, on March 14, 1903, and arrived in Quebec on May 13, 1903. He arrived back home to Wittenburg, Nova Scotia, May 14, 1903. I would sit out on the veranda at my grandparents' house on warm evenings and listen to him tell me about every step along the way. I was so thrilled to be there and listen. He had a very soft voice, and I had to get up real close to hear each and every word. I would later learn from my younger cousins that they all wished they could have heard the story firsthand. He had a pipe that he smoked, and I would try to inhale some of it when he would get close to me. I have been to the old house many times, and the veranda is one of my favorite spots. I can almost smell the tobacco smoke when I go there.

Listening to people like my dad, my grandfather, along with many others was far greater than any material gift I could have received. We spend most of our life working hard trying to gain material things to make us happy, yet the smell of fresh pipe tobacco smoke on a cold frosty day or the smell of roses in early summer can give us so much more joy. Life is full of pleasures, yet in our haste, we pass them by.

Sometimes we become so focused on the finish line that we fail to find joy in the journey.

As I reach the end of this little journey, I am pleased that I persevered and have finally reached the last pages. While writing, I found that my mind seemed to open up and I remembered so many things that would normally be lost. I have so many people to thank for my journey this far and for the encouragement I received. I want to make special mention of a few of my relatives who have had a huge influence on my life and are no longer here with us.

My father, Clifford Joseph Taylor. To me, he was a giant. He did everything a son could ask his father to do. I miss our fishing trips the most. When I was about seven years old, I played hooky one day and went fishing with my brother Malcolm. It was really his idea as school was not one of his top priorities. When my father found out that evening, he was quite upset and told me so. Several years later, when I was in high school, my dad said to me, "How are your marks in school?" When I told him I was doing well, he said, "How would you like to go fishing with me tomorrow?"

We went the next day, which was a school day. He made it a point to ask me to go with him once a year for several years after that. I always looked forward to that little fishing trip. The number of fish we caught did not matter. The time together was so special. He always caught more fish than I did, but somehow the largest fish ended up in my bag. When we got home, he would always say, "Robert got the biggest fish." I will never forget the last trip we had. He had been feeling bad for quite some time. I drove from town one day to take him to a small lake quite handy to the road. He was a little reluctant to go, but I convinced him it would be good for him. When we arrived, I took him right to the edge of the lake. I even brought him a chair to give him more comfort. After we were there just a short time, I noticed he was just watching the lake and he seemed like his mind was in another place. I asked him if he would like to go home, and he smiled and said, "The fish probably would not taste good anyway." It was sad for me, but I realized our dad was tired and his home was the place to be.

Shortly before this, he got a call from a heart specialist in Halifax requesting a visit to his office. They wanted him there for a much-needed heart examination. He told me he did not think he wanted to go all the way to Halifax. I told him I would drive up, pick him up, take him to town, and have him back that afternoon. He decided he would go, but reluctantly. When I picked him up, he seemed much quieter than usual. He had his pipe but never touched it all the way to town. We arrived at the doctor's office at 3:00 p.m. on the dot. I went in while they gave him a complete examination.

After the doctor was finished, he told my father he was in fine shape for his age. Dad asked him if it would be okay if he smoked a little. The doctor asked him if he smoked a little now. He said, "Yes, once in a while." The doctor said, "That is fine, just once in a while." Then Dad asked him if a little drink would hurt him. The doctor said, "Do you drink a little now?" "Just a little," he said. The doctor said, "That is okay too if you drink just a little." When we left the office and got in the car, he lit up his pipe. His next words were, "Where's the liquor store?" He never stopped talking all the way home that evening. That doctor gave him a reason to live a little longer.

When he did get too weak to get out of bed and we took him to the hospital, he was still our funny dad. One of the nurses was putting a sheepskin under him to make him a little more comfortable. When she did this, he wanted to know if it was a ram or a ewe. He never had a lot of material things. I never heard him ask for anything, but he sure gave a lot. Yeah, he was a special dad.

My wish has been to make my three sons as proud of me as I have been of my dad.

My mother, Jean MacLean Stewart, was certainly very special to me and all of our family. Our time together was very short, but we had quality time and I learned so much from her. I remember combing her long hair and probably being a nuisance, but if I was, she never complained. She loved all of her children, and I am very fortunate to be one of them.

My great aunt Martha was another one of my special people. She had a way of making you do things you did not want to do, but you did it anyway and with a smile on your face. She treated me so well at a time I needed it so much. She comes to my mind almost every day. I can't remember visiting anyone else that gave me as much joy. As we go through life, we meet people that we don't see very often, yet they seem to have a tremendous connection to us. Aunt Martha was one of those people. If we got to see her twice a year for a day or two, that was fantastic.

My stepmother was another lady that cared for me in a special way. She was very kind to me and did everything for me a child could ask for. She married my dad who had a growing family and supported us as best as she could.

I must thank my wife Vivian for being patient during the many hours I spent on this book and neglecting so many household chores. I also want to thank her for her many years of being a mother to three growing boys and a husband that spent a lot of time on the road.

I want to thank all of my family and friends for the help with stories and support. A very special thanks to my three sons and their families for all the joy they have provided.

I wish to thank my good friend Budd Gavel for his hard work. He has done all of my proofreading and has encouraged me all the way from start to finish.

When I started my first book, I found myself wondering why I decided to take such a big step into the unknown. Would I fall on my face? Would people laugh at me? Perhaps if I were lucky, they would laugh with me. Writing the two books has given me great rewards. I have renewed strong bonds with the people I have mentioned and many others close to me. If I could offer all of you readers advice that would pay huge dividends, it would be this: Say something nice to everyone you meet. Do something nice for as many as you can. Time slips by so fast. Don't miss a chance. Just remember, any step in the right direction is really a giant step.

This is a picture of the school in Wittenburg, Nova Scotia. All of my father's siblings attended this school. In later years, my mother taught there. My aunt Roberta Taylor (Annand) did the drawing. Our dear aunt passed February 24, 2014, at the age of ninety-three. She was a charming lady, and her accomplishments would fill another book.

From the beginning as a boy until now, in my seventies, I still feel like a boy. I have tried to take you on a journey that was full of fun and laughter. Life is certainly not all fun, and we also shed many tears along the way. I wanted to tell of the positive side and leave you with a good feeling. I am sure each of you will find that this book brings back old tales of your own personal life. If this happens, I will have accomplished what I have set out to do. Thanks to my friends and family, this book is complete. I sincerely hope you enjoyed the stories. My greatest rewards for my efforts have been the flood of memories that came back to me as I was trying to recall some of the fun we had. I was especially moved when I realized just how many memories of my mother came back to me as I was making my notes. I was overwhelmed with thoughts of her and how close we really were. On behalf of my brothers and sisters, I dedicate this book in memory of our mother, *Jean MacLean Stewart (Taylor)*. We shared just a few short years on an old country farm, but they will remain with us for the rest of our lives. There were many other events that came back to me since I started writing. Memories and dreams can make great companions. I have been blessed with great friends, classmates, and a wonderful family during my school years and beyond. It has been a pleasure sharing a few stories with you. I am proud to say the tales are true and from the heart. There are no fancy words or phrases, just good old country pride.

Don't cry because it is over, smile because it happened.
(Dr. Seuss)

The Taylor family in Stewart Hill.

Printed in the United States
By Bookmasters